To

Benji Weizman

This book is for you and because of you. I consider myself blessed for having you in my life, and for all I have learned because of you.

You inspire me and make me proud!

Love,

Cláudia Cisterna

Ad Dei Gloriam

Table of Contents

Answer Key does not provide all the answers but shows examples and what could be an acceptable answer

Acknowledgments

This book would not be possible without the following people:

Giovanna Cisterna, for the illustrations on the cover and pages 83, 90, 136, 156, 157, and 219.

Marta Cisterna for writing the short stories "The Teddy Bear" and "The Neighbour."

Shirley Gordon, Mimi Martin, Martha Ould, Julia Cisterna, and Morgan Wolf. Thank you for sharing the responsibility of editing and proofreading the texts.

Jackie D'Costa for being a changemaker, and Nicholas D'Costa for being part of this journey's first steps.

Sandra Weizman, a mother who doesn't look at what is but rather at what could be. Thank you for sharing your vision and enriching my knowledge.

Erika Anderson and Amy Campbell from ACE Teaching and Consulting, for sharing their expertise. For more information: http://www.acetc.info/all-about-ace/

Soma Mukhopadhyay developed the RPM technique for teaching and communicating with autistic children. https://www.halo-soma.org/

My family and friends, whose names I borrowed to add interest to the book and those who said this project was a great idea.

About This Book

This book contains various cognitive development activities for children grades 3 to 5 on the autism spectrum. It is essential to understand and differentiate each child's challenges to help them progress and learn. Their cognitive skills vary and develop at a different rate, but they can improve over time through education, which is the first step towards a better quality of life.

Although these activities are intended for children with learning disabilities associated with autism, any child can benefit from them to help develop self-awareness and critical thinking.

Time, time, time. Work one concept at a time, remembering that "time" might be days, weeks, or months. This book is only a tool to be used as support when working towards developmental abilities. Create new activities based on the content of the book and incorporate repetition with practical learning. Use multisensory techniques when talking about scents, sounds, texture, and the unknown. Visual support can potentially improve understanding and, consequently, communication. We can use reading comprehension as an example: If the child reads a short story about sequoia trees, show images and videos from the web that supports the text. What is the smell of a tangy scent? How does it feel to touch a gritty surface?

Some of these activities are more challenging than others depending on the child's understanding but can be adapted accordingly for optimal results.

As the student progresses through the activities, the parent or teacher's role is to offer support as needed, reminding the child of previous experiences and knowledge; gradually stepping back to allow them to solve the problem. Keep in mind that these activities are not part of a test. The objective is to assist in filling knowledge gaps that would promote thought-development and independent thinking. Many of these activities will encourage the students to learn about themselves, their surroundings, and what is important to them.

You will find some of the activities repeated but in different formats.

Canadian theme.

Suggestions:

- Set the time in front of the student before each activity to encourage elapsing time awareness. Show the starting and finishing time, explaining how long it took to complete the work. The emphasis is not on how fast the child can complete the activity but rather on the amount of time that passes from beginning to end.

- If the child has not understood or mastered the activity after finishing a section, create new sentences based on that particular activity.

- Don't repeat the same activity many times on the same day, especially if the child does not understand the concept. It is better to work a little bit daily over a long period rather than overwhelm them.

- Always give feedback and support.

- Be aware of the child's cognitive level to determine what kind of assistance is needed.

- Aim for independence but guide as long as it is necessary.

- Be conscious of the child's limitations.

- Incorporate multiple choices (on paper or verbally), but no more than 2-3 options, depending on the cognitive ability.

- Don't use too many words but choose words that allow understanding, gradually increasing the variety of vocabulary.

- Some children will need more time than others. All children benefit from having a schedule. When making a schedule, include the child in the decision-making process, if possible. Set a daily goal and decide what time of the day and how many hours or minutes will be necessary to accomplish it.

- Keep the study desk or table free of distraction and clutter.

- With the help of the student, write a schedule of the activities. Add the time you start, a break time, and the time expected to end. This step helps develop skills such as keeping track of time as the child progresses through the activities.

Examples of questions to ask when reading or watching a video:

Have written vocabulary available by giving two options (one right, one wrong) if the child does not come up with the answer. Play "word of the day."

"What did the character do?" (a or b?)

"What did the character say?"

"Who is...?"

"How do you think the character is feeling?"

"Why did the character act that way?"

"What do you think this means?"

"Is the story or paragraph talking about this or that?"

"What information is important to underline?"

"How are these similar or different?"

"What would you have done?"

"How many...?"

"Where is/did...?

"Is this a...or a...?"

"What does it mean when...?"

"Where else can you use that knowledge/skill?"

"Where can you find more information about this....?"

"What else could be done?

"What did you learn?

"Is the answer in the text, or is it implied?

1. All About You

A. Personal Information

Name: _____

_____

Date of Birth: _____

> Draw yourself in front of your

Place of Birth: _____

Height: _____ Weight: _____

Parents: _____

_____

Siblings: _____

_____

Address: _____

_____

Phone Number: _____

Emergency contact: _____

Medical Condition (s) _____

_____

Continuing....

I am good at: _____

_____

I need to improve: _____

_____

I am passionate about: _____

_____

I dislike: _____

_____

What makes me happy: _____

_____

What makes me angry: _____

_____

What, or who gives me comfort: _____

_____

I know I am sad when: _____

_____

I know I am tired when: _____

_____

2. Knowing Myself.

5 things that make me happy.	5 jobs that I like to do.	5 experiences I will never forget.
1._____ _____	1._____ _____	1._____ _____
2._____ _____	2._____ _____	2._____ _____
3._____ _____	3._____ _____	3._____ _____
4._____ _____	4._____ _____	4._____ _____
5._____ _____	5._____ _____	5._____ _____

Draw yourself doing something that makes you happy using only blue, green, red, and orange colours.

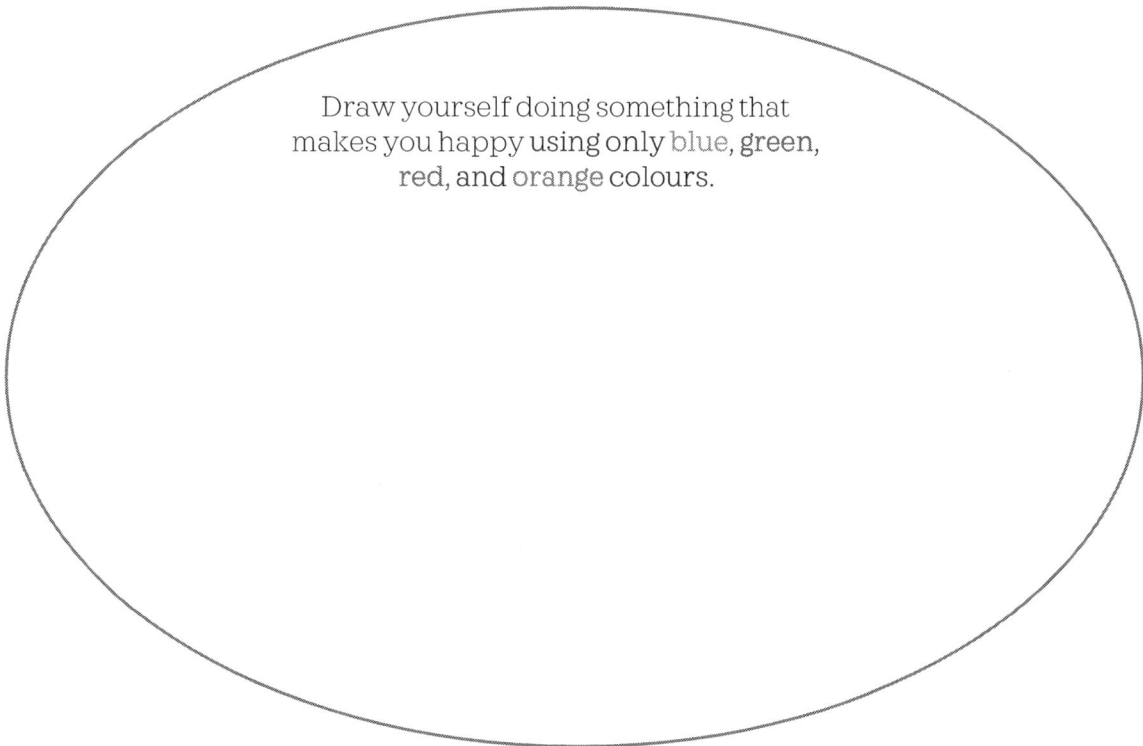

5 things s I can do by myself.	5 things I plan to do.	5 things I want from a friend.
1._____ _____	1._____ _____	1._____ _____
2._____ _____	2._____ _____	2._____ _____
3._____ _____	3._____ _____	3._____ _____
4._____ _____	4._____ _____	4._____ _____
5._____ _____	5._____ _____	5._____ _____

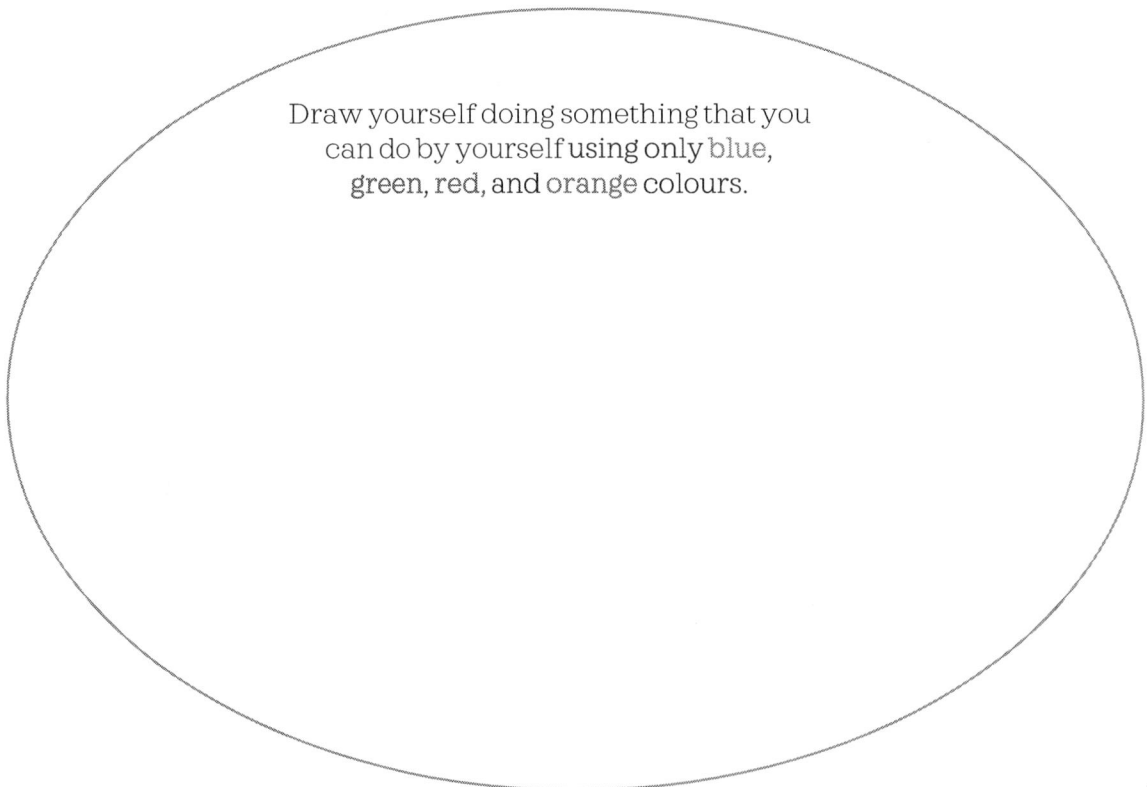

Draw yourself doing something that you
can do by yourself using only blue,
green, red, and orange colours.

5 ways I deal with stress.	5 ways I can help someone.	5 things I think about often.
1._____ _____	1._____ _____	1._____ _____
2._____ _____	2._____ _____	2._____ _____
3._____ _____	3._____ _____	3._____ _____
4._____ _____	4._____ _____	4._____ _____
5._____ _____	5._____ _____	5._____ _____

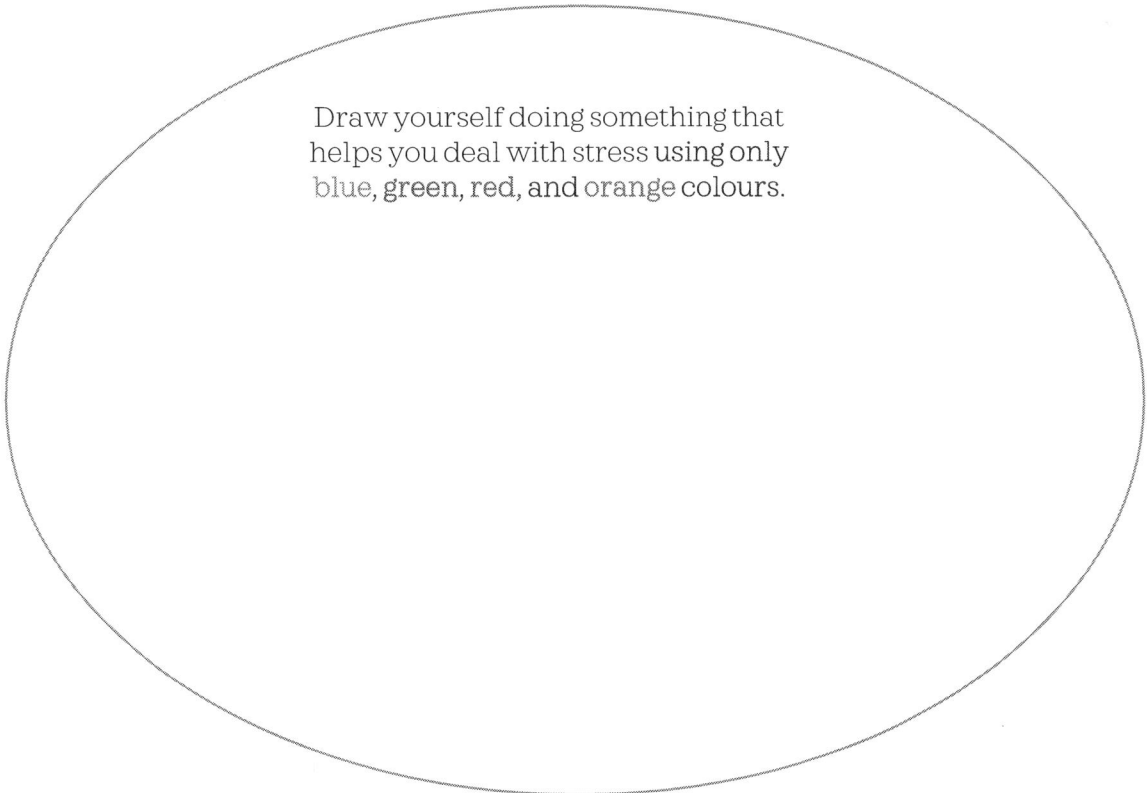

Draw yourself doing something that helps you deal with stress using only blue, green, red, and orange colours.

3. Small Accomplishment – Big Victories

A. Use this questionnaire to help you accomplish necessary activities:

Goal/Chores/Activity_____

_____

> ➤ Why does it need to be done?

_____

_____

> ➤ Due date: _____

> ➤ Can it be done before, or it has to be done at that time?

_____

> ➤ Have I done this before? _____

> ➤ Is it difficult? _____

> ➤ Do I need help? _____

> ➤ If so, who should I ask for help?

_____

> ➤ What can I do to prevent being distracted?

_____

> ➤ Will I do my best? _____

> ➤ Date Accomplished: _____

> ➤ Now that it is done, I feel: _____

B. Use this space to draw your accomplishment as if it were a comic book, step by step. Did you do it by yourself? If not, add the person who helped you.

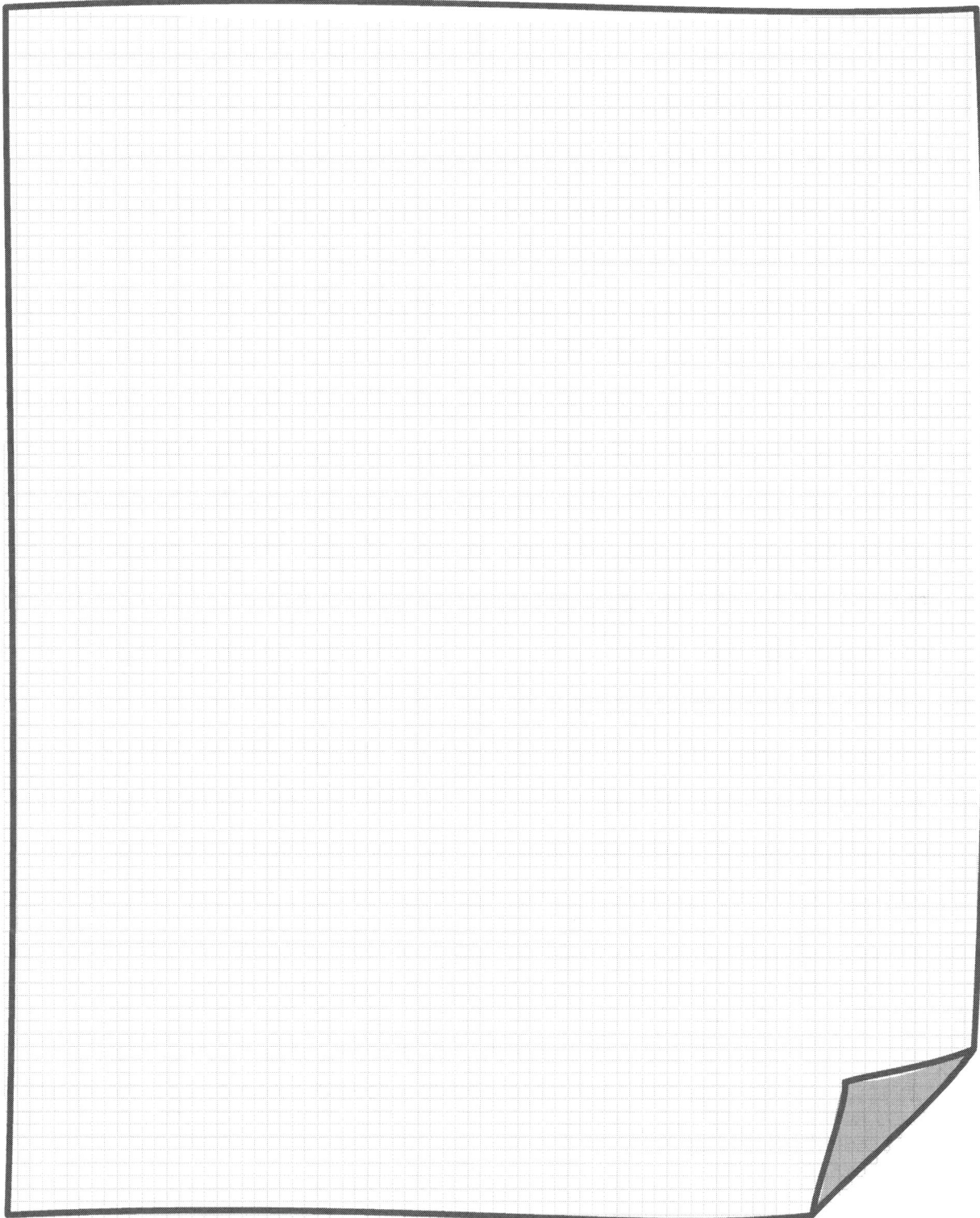

4. Self-Advocate (Learning how to speak up for yourself):

The word advocacy means to speak in favour of someone or a cause. Self-advocacy means that we are speaking on behalf of ourselves. Advocacy is related to the word *advocate*, which is another word for lawyer.

Self-advocacy is an essential skill for all human beings to have, but even more so for people with developmental disabilities. Successful self-advocacy builds healthy relationships and quality of life.

It is our responsibility to know and understand our needs, rights, and responsibilities. You might have to ask for a school or workplace accommodation or speak up when someone is not treating you with respect. When we learn to speak up for ourselves, we grow in our self-esteem and independence.

If you go to a restaurant and order a lemonade with your meal, but the waitress brings in soda pop, you should respectfully point out the mistake and ask for what you want.

Another form of self-advocacy is knowing what to do to control your emotions without lashing out at people. For instance, if you hang out with friends and something upsets you, the best option is to excuse yourself and find a place to cool down until you are ready to rejoin the friends.

Whatever form of communication you use, remember that respect goes both ways.

1. Give examples of what you should do when:

a. You need to cool off:

_____

_____

b. Plans change:

_____

_____

c. You join a group in a social situation:

_____

_____

d. You need to share and take turns:

_____

_____

e. Someone is annoying you:

_____

_____

f. Someone is bullying you:

_____

_____

g. Someone tries to harm you:

_____

_____

h. You misbehave:

_____

_____

i. You offend or hurt someone:

_____

_____

j. You are confused.

_____

_____

K. Draw one of the examples you mentioned above. Write the letter related to the drawing. If you draw about cooling off, write the letter "a."

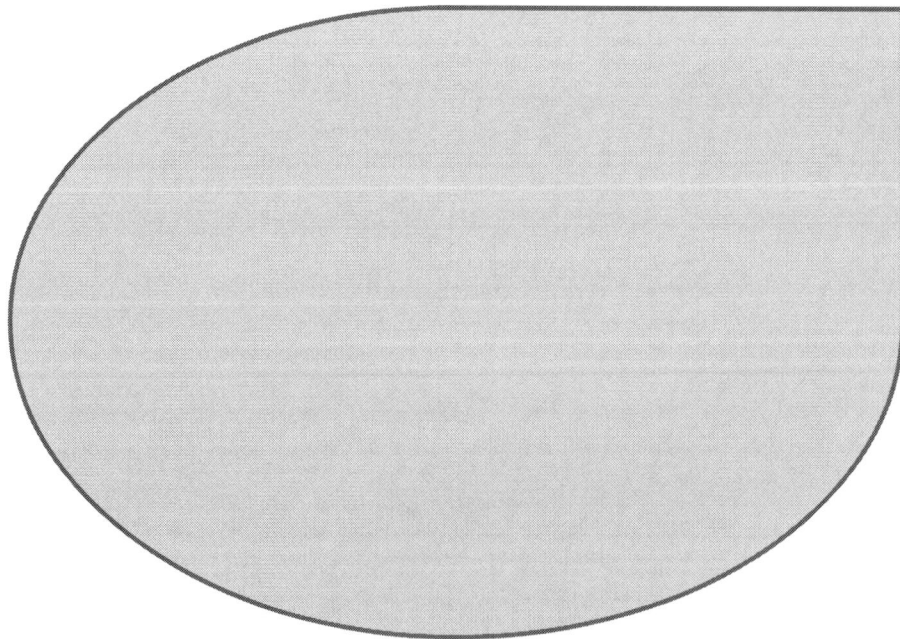

2. Give examples of when you had to:

a. Cool off:

_____

_____

b. Find someone to talk to:

_____

_____

c. Share and take turns:

_____

_____

d. Walk away from a situation:

_____

_____

e. Tell someone to back off:

_____

_____

f. Ignore someone:

_____

_____

g. Apologize:

_____

_____

h. Compromise:

_____

_____

i. Defend yourself:

_____

_____

j. Change plans:

_____

_____

K. Draw one of the examples you mentioned above. Write the letter related to the drawing. If you draw about cooling off, write the letter "a".

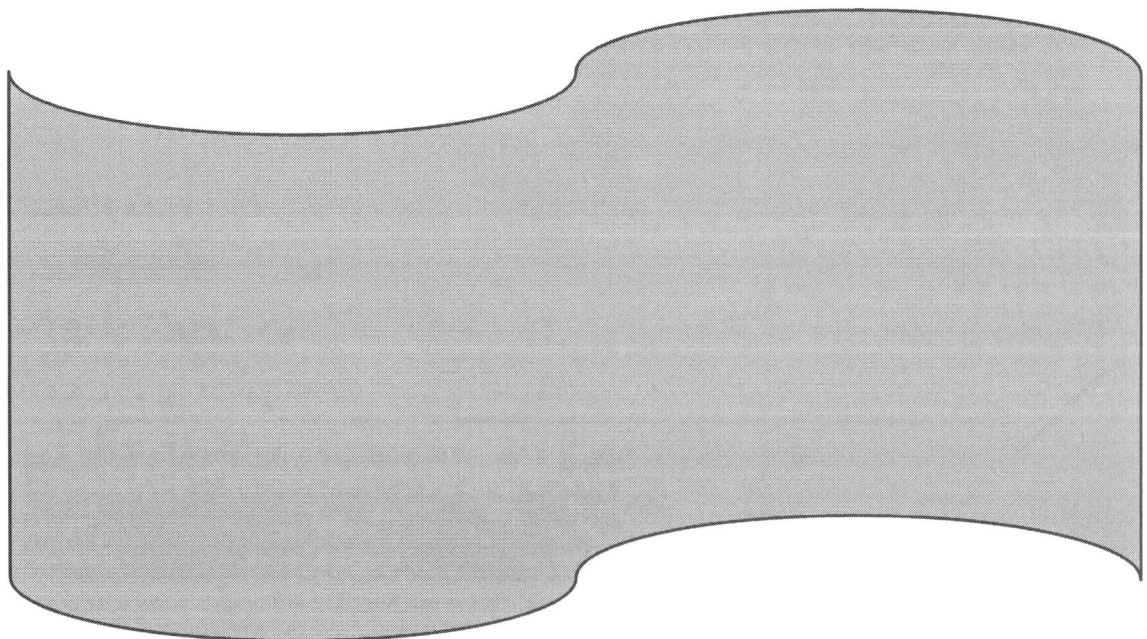

5. Relationships.

1. Do you know the difference between a friend and an acquaintance? And do you know who the people you can trust are? This exercise will help you to understand different types of relationships and what is appropriate for each one.

a. Self: First, you need to know about yourself, your interests, and your values.

b. Family/Intimate: Think about those closest to you. Some friends are closer to us than some family members. You can add your pets here too!

c. Friendship: Think about relationships that involve honesty, respect, and a common desire to make the relationship last.

d. Acquaintance: People you meet casually, maybe at a community centre, school, or place of worship. You might even know their names, but there is no close relationship.

Now that you have this information, write their names in the appropriate section of the friendship squares:

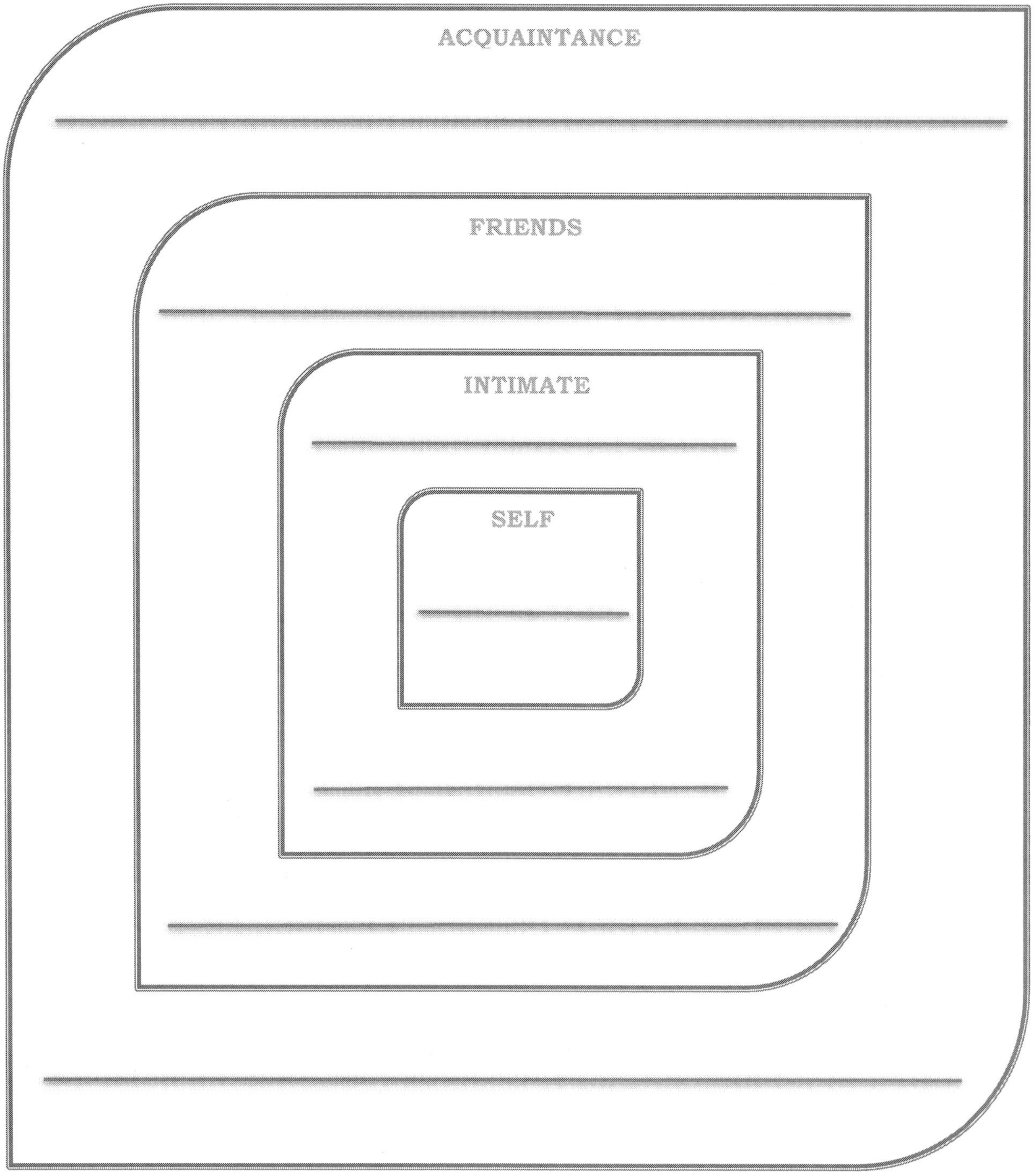

ACQUAINTANCE

FRIENDS

INTIMATE

SELF

2. What are some of the traits of a good friend?

a. Honest and caring.

b. Judgmental and unfair.

c. Holds grudge and puts you down.

3. Do you consider yourself a good friend? Why?

_____

_____

4. Write an example of a time where you were a good friend:

_____

_____

_____

5. One way of making friends is through a hobby. Do you have a hobby? What is it? Does it require the participation of another person?

_____

6. The following hobbies involve other people. Circle any that you would like to participate in:

a. Playing chess   b. Video Game club   c. Canoeing   d. Board games

e. Dance lesson   f. Sports teams   g. Drama   h. Art classes

7. When you are spending time with a friend:

a. Do you listen and respond?

b. Are you a conversation hog?

8. If you see a group of people talking and want to join in the conversation: (This is an excellent activity to roleplay).

a. Do you force your way into the conversation?

b. Do you approach slowly, listening to make sure they are not talking about something of a private nature?

9. How do you know if the conversation is private?

a. Their tone of voice is low, and they are not making eye contact with anyone outside the group.

b. They are laughing or talking loudly, and their body language is relaxed.

10. If you notice that it is not a private conversation and you think that it is ok to join in:

a. Do you wait for a pause in the conversation, make eye contact, and say hello?

b. Do you join in without saying hello and say whatever comes to your mind?

6. What Does It Look Like?

We can learn about how people feel when we pay attention to their body language. Using the search engine of your preference, do an image search of "body language examples" on your computer. Return to this activity and chose all the answers that apply.

1. When a person is nervous or anxious, he or she will:

a. Move their arms and legs freely.

b. Have trembling fingers.

c. Stiffen his or her body.

2. When a person is happy, he or she will:

a. Smile.

b. Frown.

c. Jumping up and down.

3. When a person is confused, he or she will:

a. Raise the eyebrows.

b. Scratch the head.

c. Nods.

4. When a person is angry, he or she will:

a. Clench the teeth.

b. Smile.

c. Tighten the lips.

5. When a person is surprised, he or she will:

a. Gasp.

b. Raise the eyebrows.

c. Cover the head.

6. When a person is embarrassed, he or she will:

a. Hang the head low.

b. Cover the eyes.

c. Hug someone.

7. When a person is worried, he or she will:

a. Pace back and forth.

b. Keep looking at the clock.

c. Sleep well.

8. When a person is bored, he or she will:

a. Yawn.

b. Dance.

c. Stare blankly.

7. Problem Solving.

A. When we solve a problem, we find solutions for situations that are difficult. To do so, we must identify the problem, think of alternatives, and find a solution.

1. The student club planned a field trip to the mountains, but the coordinator cancelled it because of the weather.

a. What is the problem? _____

b. What can you do about it? _____

2. While you were at the movies, the people in front of you would not stop talking.

a. What is the problem? _____

b. What can you do about it? _____

3. Every day, you sit on the playground's bench to eat your lunch, but today, another kid was sitting there.

a. What is the problem? _____

b. What can you do about it? _____

4. You went to a party with your parents, but you are not having fun because there are no other kids around.

a. What is the problem? _____

b. What can you do about it? _____

5. You were invited to a friend's house for dinner, but they served a type of food you do not like.

a. What is the problem? _____

b. What can you do about it? _____

6. You were invited to a birthday party, but they only played board games that you do not like.

a. What is the problem? _____

b. What can you do about it? _____

Colour The Image

7. Read the text, then write down the problem and the solution.

a. Jon did not know what he should take to school for show and tell. He asked his mom for an idea, and she suggested that he take the ribbon his dog won at the pet parade.

Problem: _____

Solution: _____

b. Emily had to be at school earlier for band practice, but her mother was out of town and could not drive her. Emily decided to leave earlier and walk to school.

Problem: _____

Solution: _____

c. Mrs. Anderson went to the grocery store near her house to buy pineapple for the cake she planned to bake, but there were none left. She drove to another grocery store, where she bought one.

Problem: _____

Solution: _____

d. When Robert saw the rising floodwater, he saddled his horse and moved the cattle to higher land.

Problem: _____

Solution: _____

8. What would you do

a. Your friends came to your house to watch a movie. One of them brought an extra person, and now there are six people and only five soda cans.

_____

_____

_____

b. After you finished your swimming lesson, you noticed that your shoes are not in the locker room where you left them.

_____

_____

_____

c. You are taking a test, and the teacher said that no one could talk. Your pencil broke, and you don't have another one to finish the test.

_____

_____

_____

d. You are looking forward to recess because you are hungry, but when you look in your backpack, your lunch is not there. You probably left it at home.

_____

_____

_____

9. Emotions and Affection.

1. How do we show affection physically?

a. Holding hands   b. Smiling   c. Hugging

2. What kind of action shows affection?

a. Pushing   b. Hitting   c. Giving flowers or a gift

3. Which of the following words show affection?

a. You are annoying   b. You are silly   c. I love you

4. How do you know that someone loves you?

_____

_____

_____

5. How do you show respect for older people?

_____

_____

_____

6. How do you care for our planet?

_____

_____

_____

7. How do you show that you love yourself?

_____

_____

_____

8. Write down what makes you:

a. Angry

_____

_____

b. Embarrassed

_____

_____

c. Happy

_____

_____

d. Sad

_____

_____

e. Frustrated.

_____

_____

10. Facts vs. Opinion

A fact is a statement that can be proven

True or False.

An opinion is what we believe

or

think about something.

Bumble bees are larger and cuter than honeybees.

Fact: The bumble bee is larger than the honeybee.

Opinion: The bumble bee is cuter than the honeybee.

1. Circle the correct answer.

    a. The fastest land animal is the cheetah.

       Fact or Opinion

    b. The ugliest sea creature is the manatee.

       Fact or Opinion

    c. Diamond is the hardest substance on earth.

       Fact or Opinion

    d. Copying homework assignments is against my school's rules.

       Fact or Opinion

    e. Burning the flag should be a crime.

       Fact or Opinion

    f. Toronto Blue Jays are the best baseball team.

       Fact or Opinion

    g. Lisbon is the capital of Portugal.

       Fact or Opinion

h. Vancouver is the most beautiful city in Canada.

   Fact or Opinion

i. Dogs have fur.

   Fact or Opinion

j. Dogs make better pets than cats.

   Fact or Opinion

k. The Beatles were a music band.

   Fact or Opinion

l. iPhone is better than Samsung.

   Fact or Opinion

m. Rye bread is the healthiest type of bread.

   Fact or Opinion

n. Canned food is unhealthy because it contains salt.

   Fact or Opinion

o. East Indian chapati is delicious.

   Fact or Opinion

p. Poutine is a typical French-Canadian food.

   Fact or Opinion

q. I love a cheeseburger.

   Fact or Opinion

FACT OR OPINION?

r. Milk is a dairy product.

   Fact or Opinion

s. Breakfast is the most important meal of the day.

   Fact or Opinion

t. Vegetarian diets are the healthiest.

Fact or Opinion

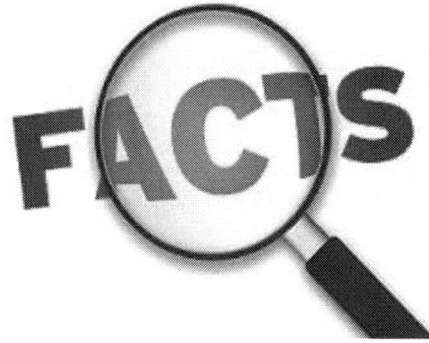

u. Quebec is the largest producer of maple syrup in the world.

Fact or Opinion

v. Whole wheat flour is unhealthy.

Fact or Opinion

w. Italian food is my favourite.

Fact or Opinion

2. Are these sentences facts or opinions?

1. Trina thinks that chocolate ice cream is the best.

Asher likes strawberry ice cream.

Kaiya prefers low-calorie pistachio ice cream.

Facts   Opinions

2. Dalhousie University is in Nova Scotia.

Mount Royal University is in Alberta.

McGill University is in Quebec.

Facts   Opinions

3. Florida is more beautiful than California.

British Columbia is more beautiful than Florida.

Ontario is better to live in than Quebec.

Facts   Opinions

4. Banff National Park is in Alberta.

   Yellowstone National Park is in Wyoming.

   The Butchart Gardens is in British Columbia.

   Facts   Opinions

5. Canada has the world's largest population of polar bears.

   Mount Everest is the tallest mountain in the world.

   The Dubai Mall is the largest in the world.

   Facts   Opinions

6. Kenzie loves hiking alone.

   Felix prefers to hike in a group.

   Finn thinks that hiking is dangerous.

   Facts   Opinions

7. The Huron is a First Nation group.

   Métis have European and Indigenous ancestry.

   Indigenous peoples are also known as Aboriginal peoples.

   Facts   Opinions

8. The largest Chinese community outside Asia is in the USA.

   Brazil has the largest Japanese population outside Japan.

   Scots started to immigrate to Canada in 1621.

   Facts   Opinions

9. Disneyland is better than Disneyworld.

   SeaWorld is more beautiful than Ocean Park.

   I prefer Tivoli Gardens than Legoland.

   Facts   Opinions

10. Peter Pan is a fictional story.

    Peter Pan and Wendy form a special relationship.

    Peter Pan did not want to grow up.

    Facts   Opinions

11. Beavers are cute.

    I think Panda bears are the cutest.

    There is nothing cuter than a puppy.

    Facts   Opinions

12. An orphan is a person without parents.

    A widow is a woman whose spouse has died.

    A widower is a man whose spouse has died.

    Facts   Opinions

13. Change is good.

    Kissing is romantic.

    Life is tough.

    Facts   Opinions

14. Physical activity can help us sleep better.

    Good sleep improves concentration.

    Some people dream in black and white.

    Facts   Opinions

15. The largest city in the world is Tokyo.

    Tokyo has more inhabitants than the whole country of Canada.

    Japanese people wear Kimonos for special ceremonies.

    Facts   Opinions

3. Notice the differences and write F (fact) or O (opinion) on the line.

1.   Ottawa is the capital of Canada.   _F_

      Ottawa is beautiful.   _O_

2.   Mary baked a chocolate cake.   _____

      The cake is delicious.   _____

3.   Justin Bieber is a pop singer.   _____

      Justin Bieber deserves an award.   _____

4.   Raw chicken can be make you sick.   _____

      Baked chicken is delicious.   _____

5.   Chocolate milk tastes better than regular milk.   _____

      Chocolate mild has too much sugar.   _____

6.   "In Flanders Fields" was written by a Canadian doctor.   _____

      "In Flanders Fields" is hard to understand.   _____

7.   Eggs contain protein.   _____

      Eggs are delicious.   _____

8.   Igloos are cute.   _____

      Igloos are made of blocks of snow.   _____

9.   The beaver is the largest rodent in North America.   _____

      The beaver is the cutest rodent in North America.   _____

10. Wayne Gretzky is a famous hockey player. _____

   Wayne Gretzky is the best hockey player ever. _____

11. Body language is how we communicate without words. _____

   Body language is easy to understand. _____

12. The Chronicles of Narnia is a series of fantasy novels. _____

   The Chronicles of Narnia is the best series ever written. _____

13. Beavers can build amazing dams. _____

   Beavers can build dams. _____

14. Diana Krall plays the piano. _____

   Diana Krall plays the piano beautifully. _____

15. WestJet is the best airline in Canada. _____

   WestJet Airlines is from Alberta. _____

16. The Great Wall of China is the longest structure in the world. _____

   The Great Wall of China is mesmerizing. _____

17. The eagle is the national symbol of the United States. _____

   The eagle is the most beautiful bird in the world. _____

18. Comets are remarkably interesting. _____

   Comets orbits the Sun. _____

19. Smoke detectors are useless. _____

   Smoke detectors are used to detect fire. _____

20. Disneyland is in California. _____

I love going to Disneyland. _____

21. Canada is north of the United States. _____

Canada is the best country in the world. _____

22. The United States is a beautiful country. _____

The United States consists of fifty states. _____

23. An iPad is a type of tablet. _____

Tablets are fun to use in the classroom. _____

4. Determine if the sentence is a statement of fact or an opinion. Then write the topic of the sentences.

1. I think summer is better than winter.

Winter is better than summer.

I prefer spring.

These are opinions about the seasons.

2. There are 365 days in a year.

There are 12 months in a year.

There are 52 weeks in a year.

3. The prettiest colour of the rainbow is red.

   The prettiest colour of the rainbow is orange.

   All the colours of the rainbow are beautiful.

---

4. Up is the opposite of down.

   Down is the opposite of up.

   Up is high, and down is low.

---

5. I love hamburgers.

   I love chicken nuggets.

   I am a vegetarian.

---

6. Inkheart is about a man who bring storybook characters to life .

   Inkheart is a popular movie.

   Inkheart was written by Cornelia Funke.

---

7. The sun provides light.

   The sun provides heat.

   The sun is a source of energy.

---

5. Write an F for Fact and an O for Opinion.

1. Water is important for our health.   _____

   Water is delicious.   _____

   Every living thing needs water.   _____

2. Calgary is the most attractive city in Alberta.   _____

   Calgary should be the Capital of Alberta.   _____

   Calgary is a city in Alberta.   _____

3. Prince William should be king of England.   _____

   Prince William is a nice man.   _____

   Prince William is the Duke of Cambridge.   _____

4. French is the most beautiful language.   _____

   French is spoken in Quebec.   _____

   French is spoken in New Brunswick.   _____

5. Italian food is the best food in the world.   _____

   Italian language is beautiful.   _____

   Italian history is rich.   _____

6. A Zamboni is used to clean the ice of a skating rink.   _____

   Zamboni was invented by Frank Zamboni.   _____

   The Zamboni is the coolest machine ever.   _____

7. Winnipeg is in Manitoba.   _____

   Manitoba is in Canada.   _____

   Canada is the most beautiful country in the world.   _____

6. Write a **Fact and an Opinion** about:

1 The months of the year.

     Fact: _____

     Opinion: _____

2. Your Family.

     Fact: _____

     Opinion: _____

3. Your Hometown.

     Fact: _____

     Opinion: _____

4. Your Friend.

     Fact: _____

     Opinion: _____

5. Music.

     Fact: _____

     Opinion: _____

6. Horses.

     Fact: _____

     Opinion: _____

7. Your school.

    Fact: _____

    Opinion: _____

8. Skiing.

    Fact: _____

    Opinion: _____

9. Hockey.

    Fact: _____

    Opinion: _____

10. Cheetah.

    Fact: _____

    Opinion: _____

11. Canada.

    Fact: _____

    Opinion: _____

12. Friendship.

    Fact: _____

    Opinion: _____

7. Draw and tell. Use the first column to draw what it suggests, and on the second column, add a Fact and an Opinion about that image. Remember, you can search online to help you find facts about each subject.

a. A castle	*Fact: A castle is a large, sturdy building.* *Opinion: Castles are very romantic.*
b. A butterfly	Fact: Opinion:
c. Car	Fact: Opinion:
d. Television	Fact: Opinion:
e. Cell phone	Fact: Opinion:
f. Soccer ball	Fact: Opinion:

8. Choose three things that you like or that are important to you and write four facts and four opinions about each one of them.

1. _____

Facts

1. _____
2. _____
3. _____
4. _____

Opinions

1. _____
2. _____
3. _____
4. _____

2. _____

Facts

5. _____
6. _____
7. _____
8. _____

Opinions

5. _____
6. _____
7. _____
8. _____

3. _____

Facts

1. _____
2. _____
3. _____
4. _____

Opinions

1. _____
2. _____
3. _____
4. _____

11. Cause and the Effect

Cause and effect is a relationship between actions. The *cause* is why it happens (be*cause*). The *effect* is what happened as a result or of the cause.

1. Write the cause and the effect of each statement. Ask "why," and use (be) "cause" to help you to come up with the correct answer.

   a. I went to the bank to withdraw the money.

   Cause:

   _____

   Effect:

   _____

   b. I am going to Erika's house to return the movie that I borrowed from her.

   Cause:

   _____

   Effect:

   _____

   c. Joey did not behave well in class, so the teacher sent him to the principal's office.

   Cause:

   _____

   Effect:

   _____

d. Caspian's boss fired him because he was disrespectful to his supervisor.

Cause:

_____

Effect:

_____

e. Isla received a gift from her teacher for good behaviour.

Cause:

_____

Effect:

_____

f. The leader expelled Rumi from her social group because she hit a member of the team.

Cause:

_____

Effect:

_____

g. The manager of the comedy club invited Finn to perform at the club because he is funny.

Cause:

_____

Effect:

_____

Colour The Image

h. When water is heated, the water boils.

Cause:

_____

Effect:

_____

i. I left my lunch at home, so I had to eat at the cafeteria.

Cause:

_____

Effect:

_____

2. Underline the cause with a red pencil and the effect with a **blue pencil**.

    a. Cara's dress is wrinkled, so her mother ironed it.

    b. Sally took out her art box because she wanted to paint.

    c. Today there were no classes because of a heavy snowfall.

    d. Soraya went to bed early because she was exhausted.

    e. Xavier was very hungry, so he ate three hotdogs.

    f. Tatiana's flowers died because she did not water them.

    g. We ran out of milk, so we made hot chocolate with water instead.

    h. Atticus sneezes whenever he is around cats.

    i. Zaylee could not see well, so she got glasses.

    j. The oven temperature was too high, so the cookies burned.

    k. Grandma is coming for dinner, so we are cleaning the house.

    l. The popcorn bag ripped at the bottom; it spilled all over.

    m. My cat is sick, so mom took him to the vet.

n. There is 30 cm of snow on the ground, so I made a snowman.

o. Brody blew a giant bubble gum bubble; it splattered on his face.

p. Fletcher slipped on a banana peel and broke his leg.

q. My dad gave me a tablet for my birthday.

r. Eugene went to the doctor because he is sick.

s. Tabatha went to the grocery store to buy cheese.

t. I poked a balloon with a needle; it popped.

u. I pushed the power button of the remote control, and the TV turned on.

v. I turned on the faucet, and water came out.

w. Willow kicked her support worker at recess, so she was not allowed back into the class.

3. Add the effect to each sentence.

a. Giba lost his balance, as a result (effect), *he fell out of the tree.*

b. I missed the bus, so _____

_____

c. It was raining, so _____

_____

d. Ruthie is allergic to wheat, therefore, _____

e. Gage was always late for school, consequently _____

_____

f. Edgar took the wrong turn, therefore, _____

_____

g. Leigh was so tired that _____

_____

h. Hadassah ate so many cookies that _____

_____

i. Grandpa was careful to climb the stairs, therefore _____

_____

j. Milo decided to have a party, so _____

_____

k. It was raining when we went to the driving lesson, _____

_____

l. The traffic lights are green, so _____

_____

m. The traffic lights are red, so _____

_____

n. Public transit is on strike, consequently _____

_____

o. The teacher left the classroom for a moment, as a result, _____

_____

p. We do not have enough money. Therefore, _____

_____

q. The weather has been very cold, but _____

_____

r. Today is Daisy Boo's birthday, so _____

_____

s. I got two tickets to watch the hockey game, so _____

_____

t. Dad's car broke down, so _____

_____

u. Mia lost her job, as a result _____

_____

v. Rocco is getting married, and for this reason _____

_____

Cause	Effect

4. Jonah wants to open a business. Write the cause for each question below, and then write a paragraph about it.

   a. Why did Jonah start a dog walking business?

      Because _____

   b. Why does he need to save money?

      _____

   c. Why did he make flyers describing his work and price?

      _____

   d. Why did he get many customers?

      _____

   e. Why did Jonah have to hire someone to work for him?

      _____

   f. Why did the dogs like Jonah?

      _____

g. Write a paragraph about Jonah and his dog walking business with the information above.

_____

_____

_____

_____

_____

5. Write a possible effect of the following interactions.

What happens when bears see people?

_____

_____

a. What happens when people see dogs?

_____

_____

b. What happens when dogs see cats?

_____

_____

c. What happens when cats see mice?

_____

_____

d. What happens when mice see a chunk of cheese?

_____

_____

e. What happens when the cheese is gone?

_____

_____

g. Write a paragraph about one of the interactions above.

_____

_____

_____

_____

6. Do an online research to find the *effect* of the following situations.

What happens if……….

1. You swallow gum?

   _____

   _____

2. A dog eats chocolate?

   _____

   _____

3. You don't sleep well?

   _____

   _____

4. You eat junk food?

   _____

   _____

5. You hurt someone physically?

   _____

   _____

6. You scream in a public place?

   _____

   _____

7. You don't do your homework?

_____

_____

8. You don't clean your bedroom?

_____

_____

9. Someone hits you?

_____

_____

10. You don't brush your teeth?

_____

_____

Draw a personal experience that illustrates cause and effect.

12. Elapsed Time.

Elapsed time is the amount of time that passes from the beginning of an event to its end.

Here is a link for an interactive clock to help with this activity.

https://www.visnos.com/demos/clock

1. *Count in increments of 5 minutes* to determine how much time has passed *or* how much time is needed to get something done. Sometimes you will count forward and sometimes backward.

1. I walk to the bus stop at 9:45 am. The bus will arrive at 9:50. How many minutes go by between the time I leave the house and the time the bus comes?

   _____

2. The bell rings at 8:45 am. It takes me 20 minutes to get to school. What time do I need to leave the house?

   _____

3. My appointment is at 11 am. It takes me 30 minutes to get to the doctor's office. What time do I need to leave the house?

   _____

4. I left the house at 1:30 pm to meet with my friend at the bowling club at 2 pm. How long will it take for me to get there?

_____

5. I got up at 7 am, and it took me 15 minutes to brush my teeth, wash my face, and change. What time did I finish?

_____

6. My lunchtime starts at noon and ends at 12:30 pm. How long does it last?

_____

7. I left home at 5 pm and arrived at the theatre at 5:35 pm. How long did it take me to get there?

_____

8. Zahra worked only from 9 to 10:30 yesterday.

   She worked for _____ hours.

9. Bjorn goes to the gym every day at 8 am. It takes 20 minutes to get there. What time should he leave his house?

_____

10. Tory left for college at 7 am and arrived there at 7:55. How long did it take for him to get there?

_____

11. The TV show started at 8 PM and finished at 8:25.

   The show lasted for _____ minutes.

12. The train ride was from 9:05 to 9:25. How long did the ride last?

_____

13. I need to leave the house at 8:55, and I have 15 minutes to get ready. What time do I start getting ready?

_____

14. The meeting at the school is at 9:30 am. It takes 35 minutes to get there. We need to leave the house at _____ o'clock.

15. The swimming lesson starts at 4:15. I leave the house 15 minutes earlier. What time do I leave the house?

_____

16. Evie is going to the football game. She will leave the house at 6:10 pm and needs to get ready 20 minutes earlier. What time does she start getting ready?

_____

17. My piano lesson is from 2 PM to 2:30 PM. How long is the lesson?

_____

18. We arrived at the laboratory at 9:30 am and had blood work done at 9:45. We had to wait for _____ minutes.

19. Mom told me that we would go to the grocery store at 5 pm. She asked me to be ready 10 minutes earlier. What time do I need to be ready?

_____

20. Oliver and Jade booked the badminton court for 6 pm, and it takes 25 minutes to get there. What time should they leave the house?

_____

21. Madeline placed the cupcakes in the oven at 3:40. The recipe says that they should bake for 35 minutes. What time will the cupcakes be ready?

_____

22. Dad took me to the embroidery class at 5:50. It took us 10 minutes to get there. What time did we arrive?

_____

23. I am at the movie theatre, and it is 2:40 right now. The movie will not start until 3:10. How long do I have to wait until the movie starts?

_____

24. Paula needs to be at the museum at 2 pm. It takes her 40 minutes to get there. What time does she need to leave the house?

_____

25. It takes me 25 minutes to get ready when I wake up until I finish breakfast. What time will I be ready if I wake up at 6:30?

_____

26. Dad went to the drug store. He left at 3 pm and returned at 3:36. How long did it take him to go and come back?

_____

27. My friend is coming to pick me up at 7 pm to watch a movie. I have 25 minutes to get ready. What time do I have to start getting ready?

_____

28. I am taking the bus to school today. The bus comes at 7:25, and it arrives at the school at 8 am. How long does it take to get to school?

_____

29. Luanna went to the grocery store at 3 pm and returned at 3:41. How long did it take her to go there and back?

_____

30. My teacher asked me to come to school 15 minutes earlier. The classes start at 9 am. What time should I be there?

_____

31. I washed the dishes after lunch. It took me 15 minutes. If I started at 12:35, what time did I finish?

_____

32. I started doing homework at 3:45 and finished at 4:30. How long did it take for me to finish it?

_____

33. I am going to a birthday party. The taxi arrives at 7:05, and the ride takes 35 minutes. What time will I arrive at the party?

_____

34. I am walking to the gym. It is 1:10 right now, and it will take me 10 minutes to get there. What time will I arrive?

_____

35. My cousin is coming to play a videogame with me at 4 pm. It is 3:40 right now, and I need to tidy up my room before she arrives. How many minutes do I have before my cousin comes?

_____

36. I woke up at 7 am, and my mother will take me to school in 40 minutes. What time will we leave?

_____

37. Lou arrived at the drugstore at 8:10 am, but there was a sign saying that the store would open at 9 am. How long would he have to wait until the store opens?

_____

38. Jett arrived at the gym at 5:30 am and spent 90 minutes working out. What time did he finish?

_____

39. Veda usually wakes up at 6 am. Today she got up 40 minutes later than usual. What time did Veda wake up?

_____

40. Quentin usually takes the train at 8:05 am, but today there was a 25-minute delay. What time did the train arrive?

_____

41. Giulia took her vehicle to wash at 3 pm; she had to wait for 65 minutes. What time was her truck ready?

_____

42. Mira drove for 80 minutes to go to a concert. How many hours and minutes is that?

_____

43. The movie lasted 100 minutes. How many hours and minutes is that?

_____

Take a short break!!

What time did you start your break? _____

What time did you return?   _____

How long was your break?   _____

Colour The

Image

2. Count by five or by ten and add a full hour and minutes to the following exercises.

E.g., I am going to watch a movie at 7 pm. The film will end at 8:20. How long is the movie?

Start at seven and count by 5s until you get to 60 minutes (7:05, 7:10 etc.), which will be 8 O'clock – this is 1 hour. Write the number 1 on the line and then start counting by 5s again from 8 until 8:20, which equals 20 minutes. Add the colon and the number 20 after it. Your answer is 1:20 minutes.

a. My family and I are driving from Red Deer to Calgary. We will leave at 10:30, and we will arrive in Calgary at noon. How long is the drive?

_____

b. The flight from Terrace to Vancouver leaves at 11:15 and arrives at 12:55. How long will the flight last?

_____

c. I love harvest time because I can go riding the combine with my grandpa. Today we started at 6 am and came back to the house at 7:50 for breakfast. How long were we riding in the combine?

_____

d. My uncle has a restaurant, and I help him during lunchtime. I start at 11:30 and stop at 1. I usually work for _____ hours.

e. Aunt Eleonor invited her friend Elsie for an afternoon tea. Elsie arrived at 3 PM and left at 4:15. How long did Elsie stay for?

_____

f. Henry took his car to the dealership to change the oil. He arrived there at 1:20 and left at 2:35. He had to wait for _____ hours.

g. Giovanna went to Theodora's house for dinner. She arrived at 7:10 and left at 8:55. How long did she stay?

_____

h. Lucas drove from London to Hamilton last night. He left at 9:30 and arrived at 10:40. How long was the drive?

_____

i. <u>Military time uses a 24-Hour Time system instead of A.M. and P.M.</u>

Search online: "Military time to Standard time."

Match:

Military Time	Standard
0900	3:00 p.m.
1300	8:00 p.m.
2200	6:00 a.m.
0600	12:00 a.m.
2000	9:00 a.m.
2300	1:00 p.m.
1500	10:00 p.m.
2400	11:00 p.m.

3. Draw your moves as time goes by.

a. Write down your morning routine, starting with the time you wake up, brush your teeth, breakfast, etc.

1. I wake up at _____   2. _____   3. _____

_____   _____   _____

4. _____   5. _____   6. _____

_____   _____   _____

b. Draw your moves and write down the time you finished with your last drawing:

1.	2.	3.
4.	5.	6.

c. Find out how long it took you to do your morning routine: 1300

I woke up at:	I finished at:	Elapsed time:
_____	_____	_____

d. Think about something that you need to do and write down the steps below:

1._____ 2._____ 3._____

_____   _____   _____

4._____ 5._____ 6._____

_____   _____   _____

f. Draw your moves:

1.	2.	3.
4.	5.	6.

g. Take note of the time you started and the time you finished.

Beginning: _____ End: _____ Elapsed time: _____

4. **Zoom Time** – Write down the minutes and the hours on the arrow lines or the boxes. Add them up to find the elapsed time.

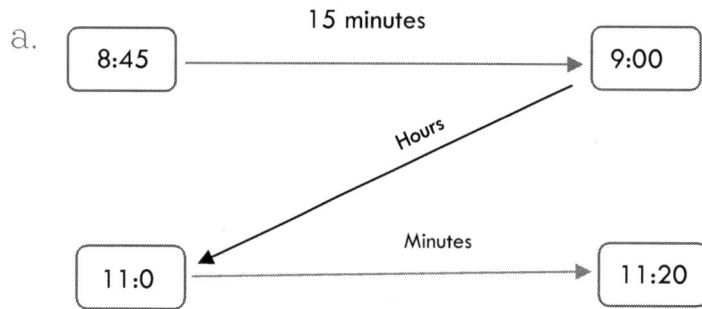

a.

```
        15 minutes
[8:45] ---------------> [9:00]
                          \
                    Hours  \
                            \
[11:0] <------------------- [11:20]
           Minutes
```

Total Elapsed time: _____

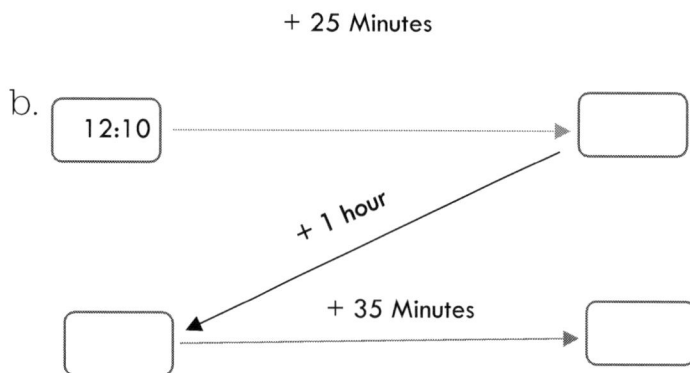

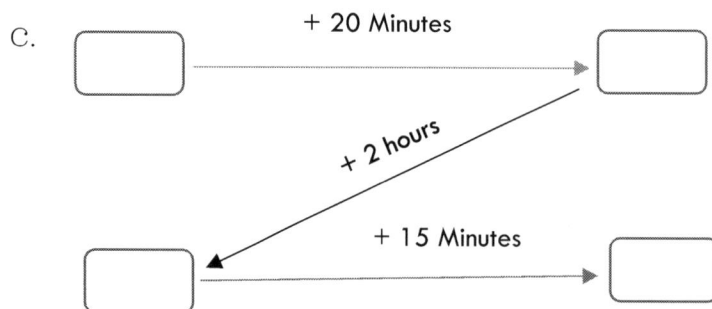

```
              + 25 Minutes
b.
  [12:10] - - - - - - - - -> [    ]
                               \
                        + 1 hour \
                                  \
  [    ] <------------------------ [    ]
           + 35 Minutes
```

Total Elapsed time: _____

```
              + 20 Minutes
c.
  [    ] - - - - - - - - -> [    ]
                              \
                     + 2 hours \
                                \
  [    ] <----------------------- [    ]
           + 15 Minutes
```

Total Elapsed time: _____

5. Back and forth (count in increments of 5 minutes).

1. It is 5:35 now. What time will it be in 20 minutes? _____

2. It is 7:45 now. (Always return to 7:45 to answer each questions).

   a. What time will it be in 30 minutes? _____

   b. What was the time 30 minutes ago? _____

   c. What was the time 1 hour ago? _____

3. It is 2:20 now. (Always return to 2:20 to answer each questions).

a. What time will be in 15 minutes? _____

   b. What time was it 30 minutes ago? _____

   c. What time will be in one hour? _____

   d. What time will it be in 20 minutes? _____

4. It is 11:15 now. (Always return to 11:15 to answer each questions)

   a. What time was it one hour ago?   _____

   b. What time will it be in 10 minutes? _____

   c. What time was it 40 minutes ago?   _____

   d. What time was it 5 minutes ago?   _____

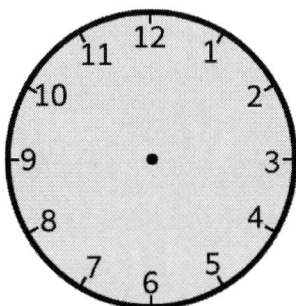

What time is it now?

Draw the large hand to point to the minutes.

Draw the small hand to point to the hour.

13. Can you solve these "Who Am I?" riddles?

1. Natural light is the best for my work. At the end of my workday, I clean all my brushes, and then I wait for the canvas to dry.

    a. Mechanic

    b. Painter Artist

    c. Makeup Artist

2. The fans began to cheer louder and louder as I advanced with the ball for a touchdown.

    a. Football Player

    b. Soccer Player

    c. Airplane Pilot

3. I am soft, fluffy, and like to sleep for a long time. When I am happy, I purr.

    a. Bear

    b. Coyote

    c. Cat

4. Humans say I am their four-legged best friend.

    a. Giraffe

    b. Dog

    c. Horse

5. I take orders and serve food and drinks at tables.

    a. Flight Attendant

    b. Barista

    c. Waitress

6. When there is a fire or accident, I drive in a big truck and help people be safe.

    a. Firefighter

    b. Police

    c. Nurse

7. I am always around you but often forgotten. Sometimes I am clean, fresh, or stinky. You can't live without me.

    a. Mom

    b. Shoes

    c. Air

8. My job is to pretend that I am somebody else. I can fake a lot of emotions.

    a. Clown

    b. Actor

    c. Musician

9. I can get filthy when I work, but my dirty job makes your car move very nicely.

    a. Driver

    b. Fisherman

    c. Mechanic

10. I spend a lot of time way above the ground. I have wings and take people on short or long trips.

    a. Airplane

    b. eagle

    c. Helicopter

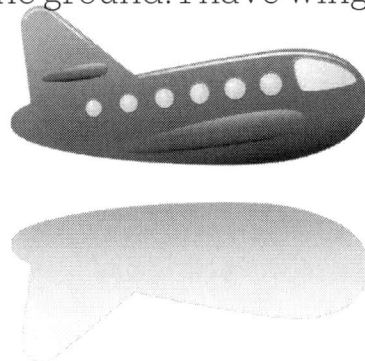

14. The 5 Ws and H

The Five Ws and H help us to gather the necessary information. They are essential in problem-solving and helpful in conversation. They are known as journalistic questions and are essential in telling a story. Search online to find interesting answers to these questions.

When, Where, Who, What, Why, and How.

1. What do you know about:

    a. London, England.

       Where: London *is the capital of England.*

       When: *It hosted the 2012 Summer Olympics.*

       How: *do you pronounce London? Luhn-dn.*

       Who: *Queen Elizabeth II was born in London.*

       What: *(is one of the things London is famous for?) The Big Ben.*

       Why: *Is the London bridge falling down? It is not!*

    b. The place where you live or where you were born.

       Where _____

       When _____

       How _____

       Who _____

       What _____

       Why _____

c. Canada.

Where _____

When _____

How _____

Who _____

What _____

d. Walt Disney.

Where _____

When _____

How _____

Who _____

What _____

e. Your parents.

Where _____

When _____

How _____

Who _____

What _____

f. Your favourite food.

Where _____

When _____

How _____

Who _____

What _____

g. Winnie the Pooh.

Where _____

When _____

How _____

Who _____

What _____

h. Hockey.

Where _____

When _____

How _____

Who _____

What _____

2. Identify the 5 Ws and H. It does not need to be in the same order as the text.

a. Skyler went skiing in Whistler on the weekend. When he went downhill, he became afraid of crashing because he was going too fast. So, to help slow him down, he did a snowplough turn.

Who_____

Where_____

When_____

What_____

Why_____

How_____

b. When Nia got home, her dog became excited and started to wag his tail because he was happy to see her.

Who_____

Where_____

When_____

What_____

How_____

Why_____

c. Yesterday, Jules decided that he wanted to be fit. He went to the gym to buy a membership and paid with his debit card.

Who_____

Where_____

When_____

What_____

Why_____

How_____

d. I went to the riding ring this morning to exercise my horse. He is overweight, so we work out for 1 hour every day.

Who_____

Where_____

When_____

What_____

Why_____

How_____

15. Unscramble.

A. Write the following paragraphs in the correct order, changing verb tense and nouns as needed.

1. Her father sent her to live with her grandparents in Cavendish P.E.I. Like Anne, she was born in eastern Canada, and became an orphan when she was young. Lucy Montgomery wrote Anne of Green Gables in 1905, using some of her own life experiences in the story.

_____

_____

_____

_____

_____

2. How is Lucy Montgomery's real-life like the character of Anne of Green Gables?

_____

_____

_____

3. What is your favourite part of Anne of Green Gables story?

_____

_____

_____

If you consider yourself a bookworm,

then you are a person who loves to read.

B. Write the following paragraphs in the correct order, changing verb tense and nouns as needed.

1. After the Second World War, he started to write children's books. His dream was to be a professor, but he decided to become a cartoonist after finishing university. However, his first book was rejected 27 times by publishers before it was finally printed. Dr. Seuss died on September 24, 1991. Theodor Seuss Geisel was born on March 2, 1904, in Springfield, Massachusetts. After that, he wrote more than 60 books.

_____

_____

_____

_____

_____

_____

2. What did Dr. Seuss want to be before he became a cartoonist and a writer?

_____

_____

3. When did he decide to be a cartoonist?

_____

_____

4. When did the Second World War end?

_____

_____

_____

_____

5. How many times did he send the manuscript of his first book

to the publishers before finally being accepted.

_____

6. What is your favourite Dr. Seuss book?

_____

Draw your favourite book character.

C. Write the following paragraph in the correct sequence, using proper punctuation:

1. My sister and I took a picture with him.

Then, we sat in front of the Magic Castle.

I will never forget my first trip to Disneyland.

Finally, we had dinner together.

My family and I had a wonderful time.

First, we went to see Mickey Mouse.

_____

_____

_____

_____

_____

D. Have you ever been to an amusement park? If so, what is your best memory of it?

_____

_____

2. First, I pour myself a bowl of cereal.

Thirdly, I grab a spoon to eat the cereal.

In the morning, I go to the kitchen to have breakfast.

Finally, I rinse out the bowl and put it in the dishwasher.

Second, I add milk to it.

_____

_____

_____

_____

_____

16. Expository writing

Expository writing means "to expose something." Sometimes a text needs to be described, explained, defined, and clarified. An example of an expository essay is the manual of something that mom or dad will assemble; it explains the process step by step. Another example is when we like something very much, and we need to explain why. For instance, I could say that I love my soccer ball, then I explain why I like it so much. "I love my soccer ball! My dad gave it to me on my last birthday. It is a Nike Merlin."

a. Write about a time when you helped someone and explain what you did to help them.

_____

_____

b. Everybody says that it is essential to eat healthily. Explain why.

_____

_____

c. What is the name of your best friend? Why do you like him/her so much?

_____

_____

d. What is your favourite song? Why? How does it make you feel? Does it remind you of something?

_____

_____

e. Look at a mirror and describe your face. Touch it and write how it feels.

_____

_____

f. Where are you right now? Look around and describe the place.

_____

_____

g. What is your favourite food? Describe it and write about its flavour and smell. What do you feel when you eat it?

_____

_____

h. Write about a good memory. Why was it good? Why do you like to remember it? How did you feel about it at the time, and how do you think of it now?

_____

_____

i. What was your best vacation? Where did you go and when was it? Describe the place. Why was it good? What did you do while you were there? How does it make you feel when you think about it?

_____

_____

j. What is your favourite subject in school? Why?

_____

_____

k. Who is the person you admire the most? Explain.

_____

_____

l. Describe the ways you help at home.

_____

_____

m. Do you prefer to live in an apartment or a house? Why?

_____

_____

n. Write the name of your favourite movie and explain why it is your favourite.

_____

_____

17. Planet Earth.

1. What is the first thing that comes to mind when you think about our planet?

_____

_____

_____

2. What is the shape of our planet?

_____

3. The Earth surface is covered with _____ and _____

    a. Clouds and land.

    b. Clouds and water.

    c. Water and land.

4. What kind of life exists in the water?

    a. Fish.

    b. Plants.

    c. Crustaceans.

    d. All of them.

5. The earth has _____ oceans.

    a. 7

    b. 5

    c. 4

Colour The Image

6. Write the names of the oceans (Search online if necessary).

_____

7. The landmasses are known as:

   a. Acreages.

   b. Mountains.

   c. Continents.

   d. Farmland.

8. The earth has _____ continents.

   a. 5

   b. 4

   c. 7

9. Write the name of the continents (Search online if necessary).

_____

_____

_____

10. What kind of life exists on the land?

   a. Humans.

   b. Animals.

   c. Plants.

   d. All of them.

11. What can we find on earth that was made by humans?

    a. Stars.

    b. Countries.

    c. Clouds.

    d. Snow.

12. One country is different from the other, even though some countries speak the same _____

13. Canada is a:

    a. Province.

    b. Country.

    c. Kingdom.

14. Canada is divided into:

    a. Provinces and territories.

    b. States.

    c. Regions.

15. You live in the province/territory of _____

16. The capital of your province/territory is _____

17. You live in the city of _____

18. Give an example of another country _____

19. Give an example of another province or territory _____

20. The capital of Canada is _____

21. How would you describe the earth and the place where you live?

_____

_____

_____

22. Look at a map or the globe and find your country and, if you can, the city or town where you live. What do you think when you look at it?

_____

_____

18. Characterization.

In books and movies, we learn about people and characters by what they say and do. Identify the actions in each activity below to understand the character's traits.

<u>Here are some traits for you to consider:</u>

Generous	Sincere	Patient	Persistent	Rude
Hard-working	Kind	Loving	Timid	Brave
Proud	Obnoxious	Unselfish	Considerate	Shy
Honest	Conceited	Selfish	Lazy	Messy
Compassionate	Mischievous	Inventive	Serious	Funny

1. Celest needs to memorize a new piano piece for the concert. When she arrives from school, she does her homework and then spends 3 hours, every day, practicing the piano.

Celest is a hard-working girl. She is dedicated to playing the piano and to school. She wants to be prepared for the concert so that she won't make any mistakes.

2. Rodolpho entered the library with his friend. He started to speak very loudly, and even though people were looking at him, he did not lower his voice.

_____

_____

3. Giunia asked her friend Lolita if she could borrow her winter boots to go skiing. The next day, she cleaned the boots and went to Lolita's house to return them. She also brought along a coffee mug from the ski resort as a way to thank her.

_____

_____

4. When Butch turned 14, his dad gave him a beautiful horse as a gift. Butch could not stop crying while he hugged the horse. He then turns to his dad and hugged him too.

_____

_____

5. Milena went to her teacher's farewell party. When she arrived at the door, she heard music and laughter. She began wringing her hands and did not ring the bell.

_____

_____

6. Faye does not mind sharing her snack with her friends during recess.

_____

_____

7. Brody went to a party, but he did not get home until 2 am. His mother asked him why he didn't come back at midnight, as was planned. He told her to leave him alone and mind her own business.

_____

_____

8. Leah told her sister to bring her a glass of water. Her sister answered that she was busy, but Leia raised her voice and said, "right now!".

_____

_____

9. Sasha spends most of his free time volunteering at the SPCA.

_____

_____

Colour The

Image

10. Every time Agape watches Bambi, she cries.

_____

_____

11. Rawan saw his grandfather struggling to get up from the couch, so he
went there, helped him up and walked with him to the dining table.

_____

_____

12. Every morning, Ramona helps her three young children get ready for
school. Before going to work, she drops them off and then picks them up
at 3:30 pm and takes them to swimming lessons. When they get home,
she prepares dinner and the next day's lunches. After washing the
dishes, she helps the children with homework. Finally, she assists them
with their bath and bedtime routine.

_____

_____

13. Marie spent the summer in a foreign country helping stray dogs find a
home. After returning to France, she received an award from her school.
She thanked the school but said it was unnecessary because she loved
animals and will always help them.

_____

_____

14. Waiola noticed the new girl in the classroom. She approached the girl, introduced herself, and welcomed her to the school.

_____

_____

15. Tao stood by the Merry-Go-Round for a long time, wondering how he could join the other children playing on the climbers.

_____

_____

16. When Cyprus' mother dropped him off at school, he kissed and said that he loved her.

_____

_____

17. Moraine thanked Mrs. Buchanan for the delicious oatcakes.

_____

_____

18. When Atlas heard his teacher calling from the playground, he turned his back to her and pretended that he didn't hear anything.

_____

_____

19. Orion prefers to be in the company of animals than that of people. He spends his free time walking with his pets.

_____

_____

20. When Raine finished baking the 20 loaves of bread for the school fundraiser, she cleaned all the baking tools and the pans, put them away, wiped the counter, and cleaned the floor.

_____

_____

21. Ragnar travelled with the school volleyball team. While riding the bus, he stood up and started to talk about all the trophies he won as a football player and how football was a better sport than volleyball.

_____

_____

22. Ebony talked about her mother being a scientist the whole time!

_____

_____

23. Brodie's boss invited him to eat at an upscale restaurant; he was dressed in sweatpants and burped during the meal.

_____

_____

24. Before leaving the house, Morena spends one hour in front of the mirror, making sure her appearance is just right.

_____

_____

_____

25. Boyd spends most of his free time playing on his tablet instead of doing homework and helping around the house.

_____

_____

26. Rhionna helped her teacher put all the books and colouring pencils on the shelf.

_____

_____

Draw yourself helping someone

19. Inferences.

When we make an inference, we conclude something based on facts and reasoning (letting your mind think and figure it out) even though the information is not clearly stated. For example, if mom comes to the kitchen and finds cookie crumbs on the table and around your mouth, she will infer that you ate a cookie, although you did not tell her.

1. Mr. Earp arrived home earlier than usual, and as he walked into the living room, he found a baseball and broken glass from the window all over the floor. He called for his son, but there was no answer, so he angrily put his shoes back on and went out the door.

   a. How was the window broken?

   _____

   b. How do you know this?

   _____

   c. Was Mr. Earp's son not home?

   _____

   d. How do you know this?

   _____

Colour The

Image

91

2. Grecia decides to ride her horse, so she put her jeans and boots on and heads towards the barn. Just as she stepped outside, she noticed dark clouds and heard the thunder roll. She went back inside and told her sister that she couldn't ride at the moment.

a. Where does Gracie live?

_____

b. How do you know that?

_____

c. Why does Gracie say that she can't ride her horse?

_____

d. What part of the passage supports your answer?

_____

3. Most people had already gone to bed when the robbery occurred. What time of the day is it?

a. Morning   b. Afternoon   c. Evening

4. The paramedics were carrying a tall person with a beard to the ambulance. Who was the patient?

a. A man   b. A woman

5. Mimi and Mulan audition for the play, but only Mimi got the part.

    Why do you think Mimi got the part and not Mulan?

    a. The director thought that Mimi was better than Mulan

    b. The director thought that Mulan was better than Mimi

6. We saw lots of Christmas lights during our trip.

    What time of the year is it?

    a. Spring   b. Winter   c. Summer

7. Most of the students passed the final exam.

    What does that imply?

    a. Most students studied for the final exam.

    b. Most students did not study for the final exam.

8. The line to look at the Pandas was
    enormous.

    Where is this line?

    a. Safari

    b. Zoo

    c. Provincial Park

Colour The Image

9. Pietro was wearing sunscreen on his face and arms.

Why?

  a. It was rainy and cool   b. It was sunny and hot

10. Kanye spilled his water

  a. The floor is dry   b. The floor is wet

11. Chris works at a restaurant kitchen.

  a. She cooks all day   b. She eats all-day

12. Tillie packs a basket of food.

  a. She is taking leftovers home   b. She is going on a picnic

13.

Zara slips and falls, breaking Nara's porcelain doll that she was holding.

a. Zara is mean

b. It was an accident

Colour The Image

14. It is scorching outside; Cassio's dad tells him to get his towel and meet him outside.

   a. They are going to the swimming pool

   b. They are going to play hockey

15. Demelza puts on her black robe and pointy hat. She grabs her black basket and heads out the door to meet her friends.

   a. It is a Bugs Bunny play.   b. It is Halloween.

16. When Jebb bites his hamburger, the sauce and tomato falls on his white shirt.

   a. He asked for a refund.   b. The shirt got stained.

17. When the woman told the children to close their books, they placed their things inside their backpacks, got their coats, and lined up by the door.

   a. This scene is in a classroom at the end of a school day.

   b. This scene is a classroom before recess.

18. Rocco placed the flour, eggs, milk, butter, and chocolate chips on the counter and greased a baking sheet.

    a. Rocco will bake cookies.   b. Rocco will bake muffins.

19. Rochella goes for a run every day after school.

    a. Rochella likes to show off her ability.

    b. Rochella wants to be fit.

20. Drawing Conclusions.

When we draw a conclusion, we use inferred (concluded) information to determine the next step. Inferring helps us to draw a conclusion. For example, your family has a good relationship with your neighbour. One evening, you see him on the driveway, and he mentions that his house was a mess when he came home from work. He said there was garbage on the floor, the foam of the sofa cushion was on the carpet, and the remote control was under the couch. Because of your relationship with him, you know that he got a new puppy, and you *concluded* it was the puppy who was responsible for the mess and your neighbour was going to have to do a lot of cleaning.

Answer the questions to help you to draw a conclusion:

1. Catriona woke up to the delicious smell of freshly made waffles. When she entered the kitchen, she saw a bowl of berries, whipping cream, and a jug of juice on the table. Beside the plate, there was a flower bouquet and a card that said. "Dear Catriona, I still remember the first time I held you in my arms, and I am so proud of the woman you have become. Enjoy your special day. Love, Your Old Girl."

   a. Who is Catriona?

   _____

   b. What meal is that?

   _____

   c. Who is the Old Girl?

   _____

   d. Who do you think prepared breakfast?

   _____

   e. Why was this special meal prepared for Catriona?

   _____

   f. What conclusion can you draw from this paragraph?

   _____

2. Faith finds Calista's pencil case in the playground after classes are over. She goes back into the classroom and asks her teacher to hand it back to Calista because she will not be coming to school the next day.

   a. Who found the pencil case?

   _____

b. Where was the pencil case?

_____

c. Who owned the pencil case?

_____

d. Why did Faith ask her teacher to give the pencil case to Calista?

_____

e. What can you conclude about Faith?

_____

3. Mrs. Kirk lit the candle as the room started to get darker. She finished her chores and went outside to get water from the well. She heated it and cleaned herself with a sponge before sitting down to read a book.

a. What time of the day is it?

_____

b. How do you know?

_____

c. Does it take place in modern or historical times?

_____

d. How do you know?

_____

e. What can you conclude about Mrs. Kirk?

_____

4. Jerrell was ready to walk to work when Franny gave him his coat. He kissed her on the lips and said, "I love you."

   a. How is Jarrell getting to work?

   _____

   b. Who is Franny?

   _____

   c. How do you know?

   _____

   d. What can you conclude about them?

   _____

5. The snow covered the land, and what once was flourishing with crops is now covered with pure white powder. Far beyond the fence, the horses gather around the hay bale feeder to get extra energy and stay warm. What can you conclude from this paragraph?

      a. It is wintertime on a farm.

      b. It is summertime on a farm.

      c. The horses are fat.

      d. The fence is broken.

21. Draw Conclusions from Images.

Look for clues in these pictures to find out what is going on. By using contextual clues, you will increase your reading comprehension skills.

What do you see?

_____

_____

What is this girl's mood?

_____

_____

The cat is chasing her. Does that mean she is afraid of the cat?

_____

_____

What kind of place is this?

_____

_____

How many people are in this picture?

_____

How old to you think they are?

_____

_____

What kind of place is this?

_____

What is in the background?

_____

What is happening?

_____

_____

Do you think the person will give the hotdog to the dog or he is just

teasing him?

_____

_____

Should dogs eat human food?

_____

_____

What kind of place do you think this is?

_____

_____

Why do people go to places like this one?

_____

_____

Who is the girl playing to?

_____

_____

22. Predicting.

Making predictions can make a story more exciting and fill the reader with anticipation. The reader makes an educated guess by combining personal experiences with clues from a text. It is a way of envisioning what will happen next in the story. For example, if your teacher leaves the classroom and returns holding a soccer ball and a whistle, you can predict that the teacher will be taking the students to play soccer. Pay attention to clues, and you will have a lot of fun!

1. Giuseppe's mother told him to close his window before leaving for school because the weather forecast said it would rain, but he completely forgot about it.

a. What do you think will happen next?

_____

b. What is the clue in the text?

_____

Colour

This

Picture

2. Gustavo was standing on a balance beam, ready to jump, when he lost his balance.

a. What do you think will happen next?

_____

b. What is the clue in the text?

_____

3. Chiara prepared some cookies and placed them in the oven to bake. She went into her bedroom and forgot all about the cookies in the oven.

a. What do you think will happen next?

_____

b. What is the clue in the text?

_____

4. Marlow has a final exam coming up on Monday. He spent the whole weekend making notes and reading textbooks.

a. What do you think will happen next?

_____

b. Why do you think that?

_____

5. While she was playing in the yard, Aberdeen's puppy ran to the pool.

a. What do you think will happen next?

_____

b. What is the clue in the text?

_____

6. Vlad walked into the building but did not see the wet floor sign right in front of him.

a. What do you think will happen next?

_____

b. What is the clue in the text?

_____

7. The bride entered the ballroom with her new husband and walked by the pedestal with a vase full of flowers on it. When he turned her to face him, her feet hit the pedestal.

a. What do you think will happen next?

_____

b. What is the clue in the text?

_____

Colour

This

Picture

8. Mrs. Burnaby removed the roast from the oven, placed it on the counter, and left the kitchen. Ruella, the cat, attracted by the smell of roasted meat, jumped on the counter.

a. What do you think will happen next?

_____

b. What is the clue in the text?

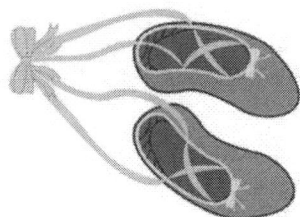

_____

9. Pablo took all the money he received for his birthday and went to the bike store.

a. What do you think will happen next?

_____

b. What is the clue in the text?

_____

10. Halie placed her leotard and pointe shoes in the backpack and headed out the door.

a. What do you think will happen next?

_____

b. What is the clue in the text?

_____

23. Irony.

Irony is the opposite of what we expect to happen, and it can be funny or tragic. For example, you run to catch the bus and miss it by two seconds, that's not ironic — unless the reason you're late is that you were bragging about how you wouldn't miss the bus.

A. Identify the irony in the following sentences.

1. The owner of the restaurant can't cook a decent meal.

   _____

   _____

2. The cleaning lady's house is a mess.

   _____

   _____

3. The fire station burned down.

   _____

   _____

4. The traffic officer received a parking ticket.

   _____

   _____

5. The pilot is afraid of heights.

   _____

   _____

6. The ice cream was as soft as rock.

   _____

   _____

7. Mark said to me, "Go and break a leg."

_____

_____

8. Jan saw the polluted river and said, "Nice clean water you have here."

_____

_____

9. Mary is a great singer. She sings like a crow.

_____

_____

10. The directions were as clear as mud.

_____

_____

<u>Add a drawing to this image to make it ironic.</u>

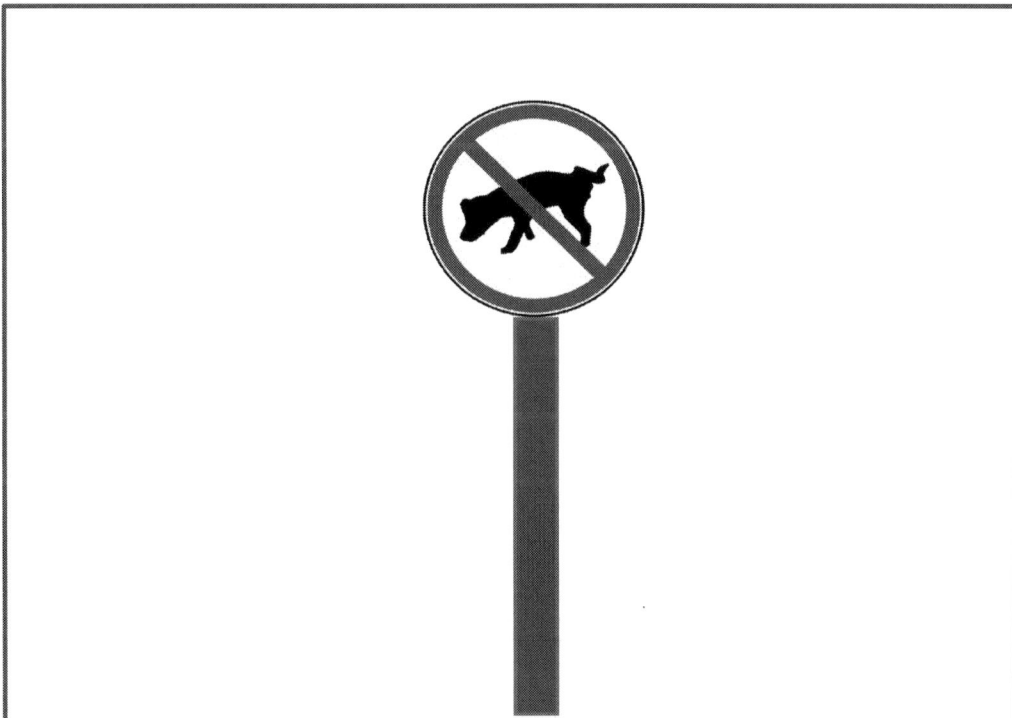

24. Sarcasm

Sarcasm is a form of verbal irony to poke fun at something. Sarcastic people use a specific tone of voice and words that mean something completely different. Not everybody appreciates sarcasm, but it is helpful to learn about it to understand it better.

A. Identify the sarcasm in the following sentences:

1. Nara's mother arrived home from work and found her watching TV. She looked around the house and said, "I am so glad you cleaned the house!".

_____

_____

2. Piper got home and said, "I had a wonderful day! I crashed the car and lost my job".

_____

_____

3. Veronica went to the mountains over the weekend, but it was raining non-stop. She said, "What a wonderful way to spend the weekend."

_____

_____

4. Antoinette sipped the lemonade and said, "I am glad you didn't put sugar in it."

_____

_____

5. Christmas break is too long; I want to go back to school.

_____

_____

6. Roan spilled the milk on the counter and said to himself, "Nice job Roan."

_____

_____

7. When Lorna dropped the laptop, her brother said, "Wow, great job."

_____

_____

8. When Conroy showed his pet snake to his girlfriend, she cringed and said, "That is the cutest snake I have ever seen."

_____

_____

Sometimes our words do not match our emotions. What is the sarcasm in this image?

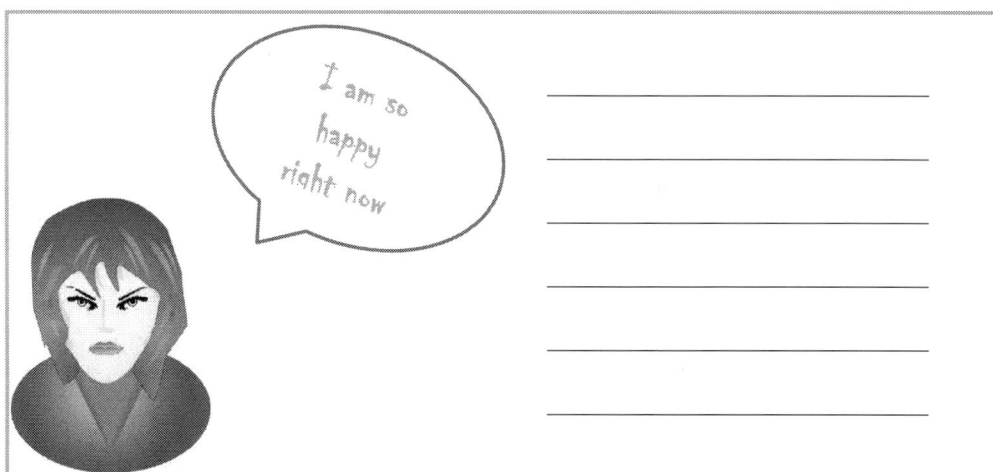

B. Sarcasm breakdown:

Millicent was explaining to her friend Opal how to complete a difficult math problem. Millicent frowned when she realized that Opal was not paying attention to anything she had said. She threw up her arms and huffed, "I love it when you sit there and listen to everything I say!"

a. Write down two examples of body language in the paragraph:

1. _____

2. _____

b. Using a sarcastic tone of voice, say out loud,

"I love it when you listen to everything I say!"

c. Does Millicent's body language match the words she is saying? Explain.

_____

_____

d. What was Millicent really saying to Opal?

1. She was happy to help Opal.

2. She was frustrated with Opal's disinterest.

e. How could Millicent express her frustration to Opal without sarcasm?

_____

_____

f. Is huffing and throwing the arms consistent with the sentiment of love?

_____

_____

25. Sentence Writing.

1. Complete the following sentences using at least five words and adding punctuation.

a. Ben does not like to drive to work _____

_____

b. I don't have anything _____

_____

c. Tom is going to Toronto _____

_____

d. Gina can't find her eyeglasses _____

_____

e. I am not sure what I should do _____

_____

f. When Mary arrived from school _____

_____

g. Mrs. Johnson was not impressed with _____

_____

h. Do you know when _____

_____

i. What a wonderful _____

_____

j. Bea and Boris are going _____

_____

k. When I left for school this morning _____

_____

l. Bob and Marley have decided _____

_____

m. I would never _____

_____

n. Maybe we should _____

_____

o. If the weather _____

_____

2. Write the first part of the following sentences, adding punctuation as needed. As you read the second part, try to imagine a situation that will help you complete the assignment.

a. _____

so, she decided to make candied apples to sell.

(Who is she, and why would she make candied apples?)

b. _____

because he cheers her up.

(Who is she, and who is he? What are her thoughts about him?)

c. _____

I will call the club to find out.

d. _____

but John prefers hamburgers.

e. _____

because he does not like to go out.

f. _____

there is no school tomorrow.

g. _____

then, he went for a jog.

h. _____

even though I was tired.

i. _____

so, he went to buy popcorn.

j. _____

unless she doesn't show up.

k. _____

because she had lost her job.

l. _____

which is in Singapore.

m. _____

you can come after that.

n. _____

the sun went down.

o. _____

I will take it out of the oven.

p. _____

she prefers volleyball.

q. _____

whenever they go to Mexico.

r. _____

she will stay with me.

s. _____

make sure to bring some food.

t. _____

but they did not enjoy the rough sea.

Colour This Image

3. Complete the following sentences using at least five words, with a cause, adding punctuation as needed.

a. Josh went to *the mall to buy new sunglasses*. (To purchase new sunglasses is the cause).

b. I gave a bracelet to_____

_____

c. Each one of us should prepare_____

_____

d. It was a cold night_____

_____

e. When we arrived at the garden_____

_____

f. I left the house_____

_____

g. Arthur arrived_____

_____

h. Phoebe bought ice-cream_____

_____

i. Ryker went to the Saddledome_____

_____

j. Cora had to find another _____

_____

k. Rumi was late _____

_____

l. The Doctor put a cast _____

_____

m. Some children have _____

_____

n. Ophelia had to _____

_____

o. Sebastian baked _____

_____

p. The boat moved _____

_____

q. Axel ate all _____

_____

r. You will be _____

_____

s. Willa melted _____

_____

t. The soccer field _____

_____

u. Milo placed an order _____

_____

v. The farmer put out _____

_____

Colour

This

Picture

4. Write a paragraph about some people who invited friends to have dinner with them. But before you write it, answers these questions:

a. Who are the people (names, parents, relatives etc.)

_____

_____

b. Why did they invite friends over? (Birthday, Christmas, Hanukkah)

_____

_____

c. Who is making dinner? (take out, homemade)

_____

_____

d. Who are the friends? (best friends, co-workers, neighbours)

_____

e. Where will they eat? (kitchen, living room, backyard)

_____

_____

f. When will the friends come? (date, time)

_____

_____

Now, put this information together:

_____

_____

_____

_____

_____

_____

5. Write a four-sentence dialogue (two people talking) where Jane and Elizabeth talk about Mr. Brewster and how much they admire him. Use quotation marks to identify the words they are saying.

E.g., "_Mr. Brewster is an excellent teacher,_" said Jane.

_____

_____

_____

_____

_____

6. Compound adjective:

    a. A hotel that is rated five stars: ____ A five-stars hotel. _____

    b. A job that is part time _____

    c. A computer that is brand new _____

    d. A shirt that is worn out _____

    e. A girl that is good looking _____

    f. A man with gray hair _____

    g. A kid that is well behaved _____

    h. A dog with blue eyes _____

    i. A child that was born first_____

    j. A player with long leg_____

7. Write a sentence using compound adjectives:

1. Chocolate-covered caramel.

_____

_____

2. Glossy coil-bound notebook.

_____

_____

3. Two-metre-long marble table.

_____

_____

4. Bright-lit room.

_____

_____

5. One-way street.

_____

_____

6. Well-known celebrity.

_____

_____

7. Hands-free device.

_____

_____

8. Ten-year-old cat.

_____

_____

9. All-inclusive resort.

_____

_____

10. Well-deserved award.

_____

_____

11. Sun-tanned boy.

_____

_____

12. Cross-country skiing.

_____

_____

13. World famous piano player.

_____

_____

14. Short-haired dog.

_____

_____

8. Complete the sentences, focusing on the underlined word:

a. I sent him an email with the <u>homework</u> assignment attached to it. <u>It is due tomorrow.</u>

b. Kevin bought a <u>souvenir </u>for his mom when he went to the museum.

_____

_____

c. Amber loved the <u>potatoes </u>her mother served at supper.

_____

_____

d. When Mrs. Fox went to the grocery store, she offered her neighbor a ride.

_____

_____

e. My <u>dog</u> drinks a lot of water.

_____

_____

f. My grandmother baked a <u>cake</u> for me today.

_____

_____

g. I received an <u>email</u> from my teacher today.

_____

_____

h. The cowboy was riding his <u>horse</u>.

_____

_____

i. Sometimes I don't want to go to <u>school</u>.

_____

_____

Colour

This

Picture

j. Joel, Owen, and Giovanna went <u>snowshoeing</u> today.

_____

_____

9. Without mentioning yourself or people you know, complete the sentences below. Remember to add proper punctuation.

a. The storm grew, gaining power with every passing hour.

_____

_____

b. Inside the cabin, Tony lit a small candle

_____

_____

c. The sunset was beautiful today

_____

_____

d. Lina's eyes are brown, and her hair is shiny

_____

_____

e. When the alarm went off, I did not want to get up

_____

_____

f. The waves crashed along the shore

_____

_____

g. His house had two windows, one on either side of the door

_____

_____

h. Julia loves horses

_____

_____

i. Marta is very intuitive

_____

_____

j. Luisa loves to write books

_____

_____

k. The weather today is very cold

Colour This Picture

10. Complete the sentences adding details.

a. When I looked up, my jaw dropped because up on the tree was

_____

_____

b. Under the grassy pastures of the ranch, deep into the ground, lived a

_____

_____

c. That night, the curtains on the window started to move like the wind was blowing them out; _____

_____

d. The pencil box started to jump up and down on my desk, _____

_____

e. As soon as the teacher opened the classroom door, _____

_____

f. I was alone in the house and there was no electricity _____

_____

g. Aunt Jocelyn was not pleased with the flying chair, _____

_____

h. Moriah opened her eyes to see the floating blue light coming from the drawer, _____

_____

11. We give the words, and you create a sentence.

1. Marathon, pain, even though.

Kevin ran the marathon even though he had pain in his leg.

2. Camping, rain, weekend.

_____

3. Scary movie, comedy, prefer.

_____

4. Hungry, fast-food, healthy.

_____

5. People, goodbye, airport.

_____

6. Handshake, friend, introduce.

_____

7. Clothing, uncomfortable, heat.

_____

8. Mother, worried, outside.

_____

9. Hurt, stone, throw.

_____

12. Conjunctions in a sentence.

a. <u>After</u> we heard the thunder_____

_____

b. After the sun rose_____

_____

c. _____
after that, we became good friends.

d. _____
so I had to cancel my trip.

e. If I *could* buy a car, _____

_____

f. If there is anything I can do to help, _____

_____

g. Once I have the answer from my teacher, _____

_____

h. While we waited for our food, _____

_____

13. Complete the sentences below using *facts from your life*:

1. I was really surprised when _____

_____

2. In my opinion, _____

_____

3. As a child I, _____

_____

4. As soon as _____

_____

5. If I could have a wish, _____

_____

6. I am happier _____

_____

7. Someday I am going to _____

_____

8. Let me tell you about _____

_____

9. Did you know _____

_____ ?

10. I remember _____

_____

11. Tomorrow I _____

_____

12. My house _____

_____

13. I amaze myself _____

_____

13. It is difficult _____

_____

14. I wish I could _____

_____

15. In the morning _____

_____

16. In the evening _____

_____

17. The other day _____

_____

18. My best friend _____

_____

19. Let me tell you about _____

_____

20. Would you like to hear about _____

_____?

21. It was amazing to read _____

_____

22. It was interesting to learn about _____

_____

23. Sometimes _____

_____

24. Everybody knows that _____

_____

25. I need_____

_____

26. When I _____

_____

27. For me, sports _____

_____

28. My opinion about Canada _____

_____

29. One place I would _____

_____

30. If I could _____

_____

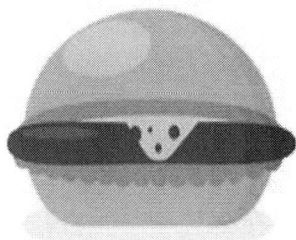

14. In Between

A. Write what happens between the sentences.

Imagine what happened between sentence one and sentence three and create a sequence. e.g.:

1. Benji opened the door to greet the caller.

He invited the guest to come inside.

They chatted in the living room for a while.

2. Ayrton went to the movies.

_____

He likes it with lots of butter.

3. Jenny went outside without a jacket to clean the snow,

_____

She went back inside the house to put her jacket on.

4. Bob noticed that there was dust on his desk.

_____

Bob prefers to work at a clean desk.

5. Sandra woke up at 7 a.m.

_____

At 7:20, she was eating breakfast.

6. Jolene needs to buy winter boots.

_____

Now, she can walk in the snow without getting her feet cold.

7. Gabe noticed that there was no onion for a dish he wanted to prepare.

_____

Gabe is now busy chopping onions and other vegetables.

8. Aviva is coming over for dinner.

_____

She enjoyed my mom's cooking and the time she spent with us.

9. Carl bought flowers before going to his grandmother's house.

_____

Grandma hugged him and thanked him.

10. I am taking two slices of bread to make a sandwich.

_____

Then I put the slices together and eat it!

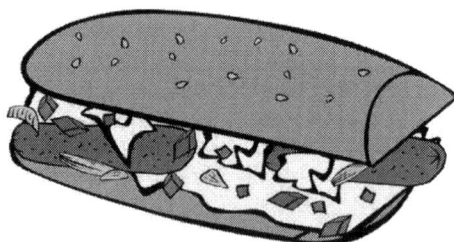

11. My brother Stephen is a straight-A student.

He had no problem entering university.

12. I tried out for the soccer team when I was in high school.

Today I play soccer for my university team.

13. Eunice needs a new L.A. textbook.

Now she can follow instructions without missing anything.

14. Betsy needs a new pair of shoes to go to work.

Her new shoes are beautiful!

15. Cristina is not feeling well today.

Now she is feeling better!

16. There is no butter to make the cake.

The cake was delicious!

17. Felipe's laptop broke down.

The new computer is faster than the old one.

18. Hannah bought flower seeds.

The flowers are blooming!

19. Paula invited Davi to her birthday party.

Paula loved the gift he gave her.

20. Jaime baked a loaf of bread.

There was nothing left.

21. Rick decided to go to the hockey game.

They had a great time!

21. The school bus did not come on time this morning.

We were late for school.

22. Jacky prepared the dough.

The bread was soft and fluffy.

23. I enjoy sitting by the fireplace.

It makes me feel warm and relaxed.

24. Romildo likes to travel.

This time he is going to Greece.

25. My vehicle needs an oil change.

I had to wait for over an hour.

26. I love hiking.

It is my favourite activity.

27. Naomi had breakfast.

Then, she went to work.

28. Andrew wanted to eat ice cream.

He chose the double-chocolate flavour.

29. Claudia likes to swim.

She goes three times a week.

30. Lorenzo went to the barn.

He went for a ride around the ranch.

31. Millie walked to the closet.

_____

Then, she grabbed her purse and went to the garage.

32. Jon was driving too fast.

_____

He injured himself.

33. Eddie was soaked from head to toe.

_____

He went straight to bed.

34. The house was dirty and smelly.

_____

Now it is clean and fragrant.

34. Becky planted some flower seeds in her backyard.

_____

They all died.

35. I went to the bakery.

_____

_____

Then, I took it to my parents.

By Giovanna Cisterna

15. Subordinating conjunction connects the relationship between two ideas. Write sentences that start with the following subordinating conjunctions:

1. Even though _____

_____

2. As long as _____

_____

3. Now that _____

_____

4. Before _____

_____

5. Since _____

_____

6. Now that _____

_____

7. Until _____

_____

8. Whenever _____

_____

9. While _____

_____

16. Draw picture and write about It.

_____

_____

_____

_____

_____

_____

_____

A House

My Favourite Place

_____

_____

_____

_____

_____

_____

```
┌─────────────────────────────┐      _____
│  Someone I Love             │      _____
│                             │
│                             │      _____
│                             │
│                             │      _____
│                             │
│                             │      _____
│                             │
│                             │      _____
│                             │
│                             │      _____
│                             │
│                             │      _____
└─────────────────────────────┘      _____
```

17. Add the correct transition word to the following sentences.

However	Regardless	Therefore	Despite	Because
Although	But	During	So	And

a. I felt Marlon was wrong, _____ I did not say so at the time.

b. Vivien thinks she is the best choice for the promotion _____
   of her experience.

c. I like cooking, _____ I don't do it very often.

d. I don't like to eat fruit. _____, I do like persimmon.

e. Her mouth was still dry, _____ the fact that she drank water.

f. Todd knew Sutton was tired, _____ he let him rest.

g. We can go to your parents' house _____ watch the game with them.

h. Laban will have his party outdoors, _____ of the weather.

i. _____ I am hungry, I don't feel like eating.

j. I was very anxious _____ the road test.

k. Pauline could always make us smile, _____ of how we felt.

l. The temperature was high, _____ she wore a dress and a hat.

m. Ainsley did not eat ice cream _____ she is allergic to dairy.

n. I ran to school _____ I arrived just in time for gym class.

o. I know you are hungry, _____ I will make you lunch.

p. _____ the race, many volunteers gave out water bottles.

q. _____ being sick, Chiara did a wonderful job at the fair.

r. This is a great idea. _____, I am not sure it will be approved by the teacher.

s. Everyone is welcome, _____ of nationality.

18. Complete the sentences paying attention to the idioms. Idioms are figurative language that means something different from the words in the phrases. If you are "cool as a cucumber," you are calm and composed. "This will cost me an *arm and a leg,* but I will buy it anyway."

"An arm and a leg" is used to describe something costly.

a. I am under the weather today,

_____

b. I think I am going to call it a night.

_____

c. Bruno has a chip on his shoulder,

_____

d. Hang in there my friend,

_____

e. I go swimming once in a blue moon,

_____

f. It is too late to cry over spilt milk,

_____

g. He was ready to throw in the towel,

_____

h. You can call me twenty-four-seven

_____

i. My birthday is just around the corner,

_____

j. I am completley in the dark,

_____

_____

k. It is raining cats and dogs today,

_____

_____

l. This is a piece of cake.

_____

m. What is the idiom for someone who cries fake tears?

_____

19. Writing with details

Complete the following sentences imagining the situation that led to this moment.

a. Books were piled (where?) *on the coffee table,* but Romy had no desire to study (situation). *We understand that Romy needs to read many books for school, but he is not feeling up to it for some reason.*

b. While dad cooked (where or what) _____
(What happened?) _____

c. Gently she (Did what?) _____
(Why? Or what did she do next?) _____

d. Unfortunately, Mariela _____
(why? Or in order to?) _____

e. An elegant dress (Where was it?) _____
(Describe the dress) _____

f. The girl struggled with _____
_____

g. It had been raining _____
_____

h. I walked to the shed _____
_____

i. Reading a book _____
_____

j. The mist over the _____
_____

20. Don't move the word.

Write sentences without moving the word that is in place.

1. Summer: _____

_____summer.

3. The grocery _____

_____grocery _____

5._____birthday.

_____birthday_____.

7._____feelings_____.

_____feeling _____

21. Who, Where, When, What, Why.

Read the sentences below and re-write them under the appropriate W.

Who   What   Where   When

The snake slithered   on the grass   this morning

1. The dog ate the cake yesterday.

When   Who   What

_____

2. These days, animals are protected by law.

Who   What   When

_____

3. Blimey sounded the alarm at the store during the robbery.

When   Where   Who   What

_____

4. Beulah danced at the club all night.

Who   What   When   Where

_____

5. Boris and his brother Bryan want to try out for the basketball team. They love basketball. Every weekend they practice at the gym, but they also practice every day in their driveway. They will keep on practicing until they make the team.

Who: _____

What: _____

Why: _____

When: _____

How: _____

Where: _____

22. Where in the text is the answer?

A. Barry and Terry wanted to go to the movies. Their dad said they could go after doing chores. First, they finished their homework. Next, they studied music. After that, they walked the dog. Finally, they got ready to go to the movie theatre.

1. What did they do after they studied music?

_____

2. What was the first thing they did?

_____

B. Adonis and Drew went to the zoo. First, they went to see the pandas, then the penguins. Next, they stopped at the cafeteria to buy water before visiting the tigers. Finally, they went to the gardens to rest before continuing with their visit.

1. Where did the boys go after they bought water?

_____

2. Where did they go before going to the gardens?

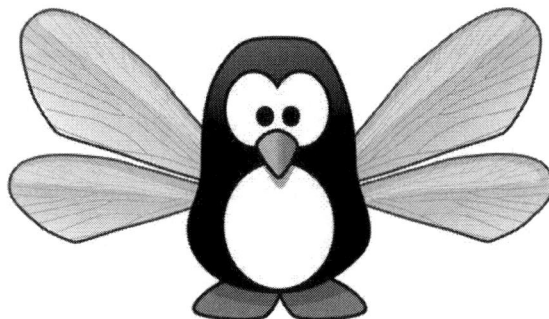

_____

C. Sir John Alexander McDonald was the first Prime Minister of Canada between 1867 and 1891. That was more than 100 years ago.

1. How many Prime Ministers were before Sir John Alexander McDonald?

_____

2. When was Sir McDonald Prime Minister?

a. A long time ago   b. Recently

26. Let us look at nature.

* Hummingbirds are tiny.

* Their name comes from the speed at which they beat their wings.

* The bee hummingbird weighs less than a nickel and is no more than 5 cm long.

* They are the only birds that can fly backward, and their feathers are very colourful.

* Hummingbirds drink the nectar found in flowers and bird feeders.

* Most feeders are red because hummingbirds are attracted to this colour.

1. Hummingbirds are heavier or lighter than other birds?

_____

2. The bee hummingbird is short or long? How do you know?

_____

3. How many species of birds can fly backward?

_____

4. What do they eat?

_____

5. What is the most popular colour of a hummingbird's feeder?

_____

6. Why?

_____

Draw a hummingbird eating from a red feeder.

27. Fantasy or Fiction?

A. Fantasy

In the fantasy genre, the author can create characters and situations inspired by real-life events. However, the characters have supernatural power and do things that do not exist in the real world. Some of the characters have magical powers, animals talk like humans, and words or movements activate their weapons. Anything can happen in fantasy.

1. In fantasy genre:

a. Anything can happen.

b. Only Unicorns have power.

2. In real life:

a. Animals talk like humans.

b. Animals don't talk like humans.

3. Fantasy stories involve:

a. People having regular jobs.

Colour This Picture

b. Magic and supernatural powers.

4. Give three examples of fantasy stories. Be sure to include the title and one or two characters

a._____

b._____

c._____

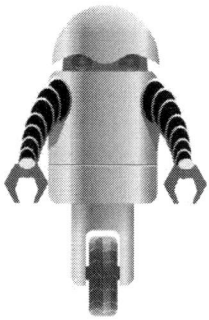

B. Science Fiction

Science fiction, also known as sci-fi, is a type of literature based on science and technology. Usually, it happens in the distant future and shows imaginary ways in which technology can change the way we live. Many sci-fi movies happen in places like the earth and other planets. People don't live like we live today, and robots and other creatures are part of their daily lives.

1. In sci-fi:

a. The story is based on history

b. The story is based on science and technology

2. Most sci-fi stories happen in:

a. The future and other planets.

b. The earth and the present time.

3. Sci-Fi stories involve:

a. Technology and robots.

b. Horses and cowboys.

4. Give three examples of science fiction stories. Include the title and one or two characters.

a._____

b._____

c._____

28. Homographs are words that are spelled the same but have different meanings.

Write three sentences using the words below, ensuring that it has a different meaning each time.

Clear (Understandable, transparent, empty).

1._____

2._____

3._____

Bat.

1._____

2._____

3._____

Fair.

1._____

2._____

3._____

Fine.

1._____

2._____

3._____

29. Let us talk about things.

1. Let us talk about the Soccer World Cup.

a. When and where will the next world cup be?

_____

b. Which country (team) is your favourite?

_____

c. What type of basic gear is needed to play soccer?

_____

d. Do you agree with the statement that says, "soccer is a beautiful game". Why or why not?

_____

2. Cars

a. Describe your family's vehicle.

_____

b. Compare your family's vehicle to your neighbour's vehicle.

Our car is _____

The neighbours' car is_____

c. Which one is your favourite? Why?

_____

d. What are vehicles used for?

_____

e. If you could buy a car today, which one would you buy and why?

_____

3. Weather.

a. What is the weather like today? _____

_____

b. What is the temperature outside?

_____

c. What kind of things do you do in different temperatures?

When it is cold_____

When it is warm_____

d. What is the coldest temperature recorded where you live?

_____

e. What is the hottest temperature recorded where you live?

_____

f. What is the perfect temperature for you?

_____

g. What is an example of extreme weather?

_____

4. Temperature

Temperature is the measure of energy used to describe how hot or cold the weather is. Temperature is measured using a thermometer. The main temperature scales used today are Celsius and Fahrenheit, and most thermometers show both.

In 1742, Swedish astronomer Anders Celsius invented the Celsius temperature scale. German physicist Daniel Gabriel Fahrenheit developed the Fahrenheit scale in 1724. They both measure temperature but use different numbers. The freezing point of water in Celsius is 0 degrees, and the boiling point is 100 degrees. The freezing point of water in Fahrenheit is 32 degrees, and the boiling point is 212 degrees. The average body temperature is around 37 C, or 96.6 F. Celsius is abbreviated C, and Fahrenheit is abbreviated F.

1. How do we find out the temperature?

_____

2. What are the two main scales that measure temperature?

_____

3. Which one do you prefer? Why?

_____

4. What is water's freezing point?

Celsius_____   Fahrenheit_____

5. What is water's boiling point?

Celsius_____   Fahrenheit_____

30. Wide Range – a variety of things to do.

Our appearance changes as we age, bringing different characteristics to our bodies. For example, a baby has smooth skin, while an older person has more dry and wrinkled skin. You will need to search for images of people online, in a magazine, or even in photo albums to complete this activity.

1. Find an image of a person's face, show it to an adult and try to guess that person's age. Look for characteristics such as wrinkles and plumpness and write down why you thought of that age.

a. How old do you think that person is? _____

b. Characteristics: _____

_____

2. Look at images of people online, in a magazine, or even in photo albums. When we describe how a person's physical appearance looks, we look at hair colour and length, height and weight, age, and gender. We also look at the eyes, nose, and mouth. Some people have scars, physical disabilities, and tattoos.

a. Describe that person:

_____

_____

_____

_____

3. Having a daily routine to help you to relax can make you feel real good! Ask someone to help you find a relaxing musical video. Search for muscle relaxation such as this one:

https://www.youtube.com/watch?v=ihOO2wUzgkc

Play the video e follow the instructions to help you relax.

4. This activity helps with concentration and relaxation. Go online and in the search bar, type "classical music for studying and concentration." It must be at least 15 minutes of uninterrupted music, but 30 minutes is better. Place a favourite book, a puzzle, colouring pages, and coloured pencils within your reach. While listening to music with a headphone, do one of the activities mentioned.

By Giovanna Cisterna

5. Body language

Watch an easy-to-understand video about body language, or type words such as "interpret body language." Roleplay is the best way to practice body language. Ask family members, workers, or friends to pose in different ways and let the student guess what they are trying to say.

6. Listen to your voice

Listening to our voice is an excellent way to make us more aware of ourselves and our emotions. If you have a phone with a voice recorder, you should find a short story of at least 15 minutes in length and record it. Then, listen to it right afterwards.

Another way is to use a recording headphone with a mic as it will enable you to read and listen to your voice at the same time.

7. Describe the image:

a. What do you see?

_____

_____

b. What is her mood?

_____

_____

c. Describe her clothing.

_____

_____

_____

By Giovanna Cisterna

By Giovanna Cisterna

Colour

This

Picture

a. What are they doing?

_____

_____

b. Describe the people in the picture.

_____

_____

c. Describe their bodies' positions.

_____

_____

8. What do they have in common?

a. Blacksmith, palaeontologist, and excavator.

_____

b. Tornado, hurricane, and earthquake.

_____

c. Fire, danger, and devastation.

_____

d. Animals, protection, and activists.

_____

e. Treble clef, bass clef, and key signature.

_____

f. Apple, stake, and ice cream.

_____

g. Northwest Territories, Nunavut, and Yukon.

_____

h. Angel Falls, Niagara Falls, and Iguaçu Falls.

_____

i. Canada, United States and Mexico.

_____

31. Compare and Contrast

When we compare things, we are looking for something similar or alike.
When we contrast things, we are pointing out the differences between them.

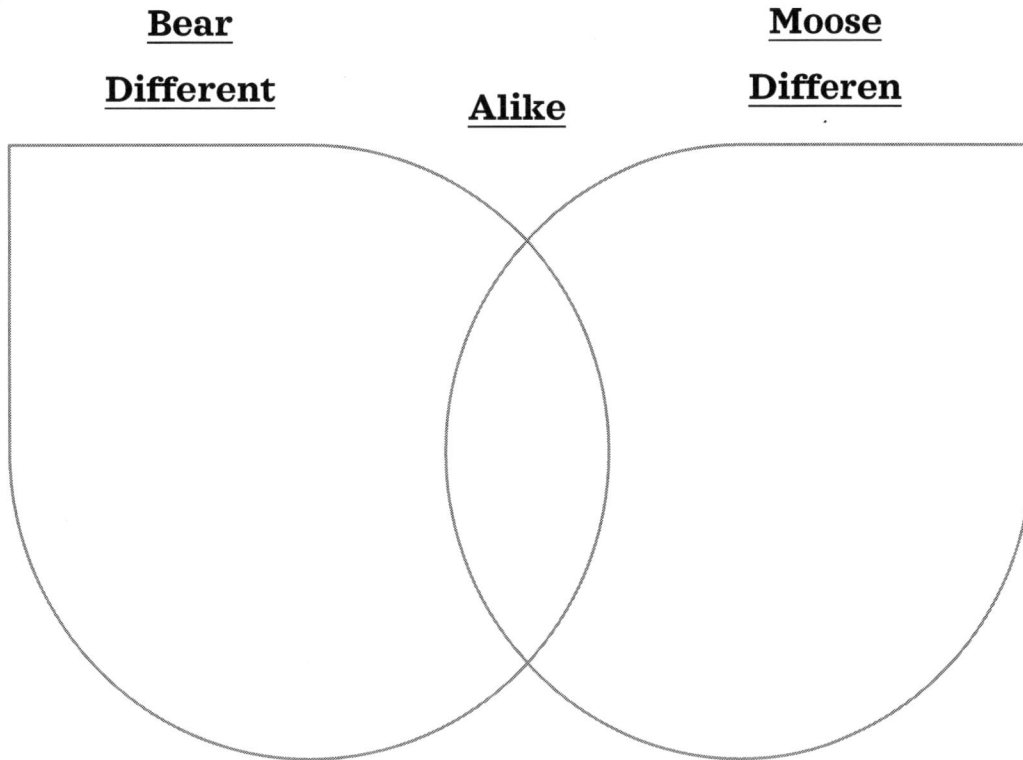

Bear

Moose

Different

Differen

Alike

In a separate paper, find the similarities and differences between:

Bicycle and a Motorcycle		Country and Province
Pig and Chicken	Mom and Dad	TV and Tablet
Ocean and River	Cousin and Sibling	Soccer and Hockey
City and Town	Uncle and Grandpa	Flower and Tree
Wind and Rain	Banff and Niagara Falls	Snow and Rain
Surfing and Skiing	Sun and Moon	Canada and England

32. What's Next?

Read the sentences below, then write what you think is about to happen. Explain your answer.

1. Cecil started to climb the apple tree, but when he was half-way up, the branch snapped, and he screamed.

_____

2. Sebastian was walking home from school when he noticed a baby bird on the ground near a tree. He looked up and saw the nest and heard another bird crying out loud.

_____

3. Melania plugged in the guitar and turned on the microphone. She then took a deep breath and looked at the audience.

_____

4. Maxine left his bedroom with his backpack and stopped at the mudroom to put his shoes on. He then turned to his mom and said, "See you later!".

_____

5. The school bus stopped right in front of Agnes.

_____

33. Retelling A Story

Many children have difficulty retelling a story. Some can retain the information but struggle to put it in order and use proper pronouns when retelling. Start with short sentences until you are ready for longer sentences.

1. "Draw the sentence."

a. The black cat is drinking water from a yellow bowl.

b. The brown dog is walking on the green grass.

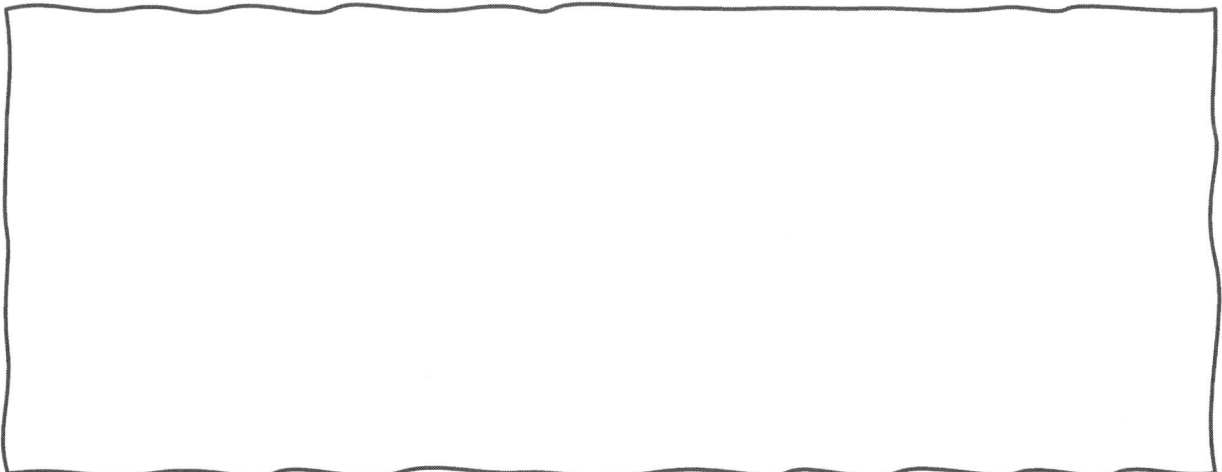

c. There are purple grapes in a light green bowl on the brown table.

d. My friend _____ is playing with a blue soccer ball.

e. I am eating popcorn.

2. In this activity, the sentences are longer. First, you draw what you read, then cover the sentence with a paper and describe your drawing. Then, write a description of what you drew. Repeat this activity as many times as is necessary.

a. The old man is standing in front of his house. The house is square; the front door is in the middle, and there is one window on either side of the door.

b. The girl is smiling, sitting on a chair holding the big Easter egg she received from her dad. The egg has alternating pink and purple stripes.

c. Mr. Zucker is fishing. He is sitting on a rock by the river holding a fishing rod.

d. An owl is sitting alone on the branch of a tree.

3. Retelling step by step.

A. In box number 1, draw a boy walking with a backpack on his back. His name is Jonah.

- In box number 2, draw a school building.

- In box number 3, draw Jonah sitting on his desk, taking notes.

- In box number 4, draw Jonah playing ball with his friends.

- In box number 5, draw Jonah with his backpack walking in the opposite direction of box 1.

- In box number 6, draw Jonah's house.

1.	2.
3.	4.
5.	6.

What do you think happened in this story? Write it down following the number's sequence.

_____

_____

_____

_____

B. In box number 1, draw a bother and a sister. Their names are Liam and Emma.

. In box number 2, draw a purple skipping rope.

. In box number 3, draw Liam and Emma walking. Emma is holding the rope.

. In box number 4, draw their friend's house.

. In box number 5, draw Liam and Emma talking to their friend Nolan.

. In box number 6, draw Liam and Nolan, each holding one end of the rope, while Emma is skipping.

1.	2.
3.	4.
5.	6.

What do you think happened in this story? Write it down following the number's sequence.

_____

_____

_____

_____

4. Look at the picture below and write a sentence explaining what is happening. Next, read your sentence and look at the image to make sure you did not miss anything. You can do this as many times as you need and ask questions if necessary. Finally, cover the sentence, turn to the person next to you, and retell what you wrote down.

_____

_____

_____

_____

_____

_____

5. Retell

1. Jim asked Martha, "Are you going to the playground?"

Retell: Jim asked Martha *if* she was going to the playground

2. Mother said, "I am going to the mall to buy a new pair of shoes."

Retell: _____

3. Owen asked, "Why do you need to go to your cousin's house?"

Retell: _____

4. I said to Stephen, " I need to buy flowers for my mom."

Retell: _____

5. Joel asked Laura, "Can you feed my horses over the weekend?"

Retell: _____

6. "Would you like to come over for supper?" Rachel asked Ben.

Retell: _____

7. "I think Hazel is an adorable child," Julia said to Giovanna.

Retell: _____

8. My teacher said, " Let me know if you need more time to finish your homework."

Retell: _____

9. "Mamma Mia is my favourite restaurant in town," Ruth told Claudia

Retell: _____

10. Dad said: "When you get home, do your homework, and clean your room."

Retell: _____

11. My friend asked, "Can we order Chinese food for dinner?"

Retell: _____

12. Rupert said, "I don't want to go skiing!"

Retell: _____

13. "My favourite sport is soccer," said Leonel.

Retell: _____

14. "I am not sure if I want to buy that toy," said Marvin.

Retell: _____

15. Lois said to Lorna, "I think that Hip-Hop is better than pop music."

Retell: _____

16. Thomas yelled at his sister, "Don't touch my video game!"

Retell: _____

17. "I want to know what time you are coming to play," Mirna asked Molly.

Retell: _____

18. "She is beautiful", he said.

Retell: _____

19. "He loves you", Naomi said Lena, "but you don't care".

Retell: _____

20. Martin said, "I am going to Jen's house tonight."

Retell: _____

21. "I think is a good idea to take Lucy with us", said Byron.

Retell: _____

22. Matt asked, "Is Gina ok?"

Retell: _____

23. Mira said to Moira, "You can come to my house anytime you want."

Retell: _____

24. "May I have a piece of cake please?", Kaira asked the waitress.

Retell: _____

25. Dad said to Brian, "You may go outside, but only until supper time."

Retell: _____

34. Reading Comprehension

A. Recall

1. Ottawa is the capital of Canada. Ottawa is in the province of Ontario.

a. What is the theme of these sentences?

   Ottawa

b. What did you learn about Ottawa?

Ottawa is the capital of Canada, located in the province of Ontario.

2. Canada has a population of 36 million people. Over 80% of the population lives near the United States border.

a. What is the theme of these sentences?

_____

b. What information is given about it?

_____

3. Over 30% of Canada's land is forested, making up nearly 9% of the world's total forest area.

a. What is the topic?

_____

b. What did you learn about the topic?

_____

4. Canada has more lakes than the rest of the world combined. The largest lake in Canada is Lake Superior.

a. What is the topic?

_____

b. What did you learn about this topic?

_____

5. Indigenous people have been in Canada long before the Vikings arrived. Indigenous people have been in Canada for centuries.

a. What is the topic?

_____

b. What did you learn about this topic?

_____

6. Canada has two national languages – English and French. Only Quebec and New Brunswick have French as their official language.

a. What is the topic?

_____

b. What did you learn about this topic?

_____

B. Sentence by sentence.

1. The word Kanata is probably from the Iroquoian language, meaning "village." Most people believe that Canada's name came from this word.

<u>These sentences are about the origin and the meaning of the name Canada.</u>

2. The western region of Canada is commonly known as "the west." It includes Manitoba, Saskatchewan, Alberta, and British Columbia.

_____

_____

3. More than half of the population of Canada live in the central region. The provinces of Quebec and Ontario form this region.

_____

_____

4. The Atlantic provinces of Canada are famous for fishing and mining. These provinces are Newfoundland and Labrador, Prince Edward Island, Nova Scotia, and New Brunswick.

_____

_____

C. Compare texts:

A. Chancey was a beautiful girl with a bad temper. She tried to control it, but it was not easy. Her mother suggested that she count to ten before saying something she might regret. Chancey is learning about self-control.

1. What does it mean to have a temper?

a. To be able to tell the temperature.

b. To become angry quickly.

2. What is an example of losing your temper?

a. Yelling at someone.

b. Being kind to someone.

3. What did Chancey try to do about her temper?

a. Control it.

b. Ignore it.

4. What did her mother suggest that she do?

a. Say whatever you want when you are angry.

b. Count to ten.

5. Why does counting to ten help you to control your temper?

a. It gives us a chance to get a grip on our emotions.

b. It improves our math skills.

6. Chancey is learning about:

a. Self-esteem.

b. Self-control.

B. Nick loves sweet-tasting food, but his mother does not let him have too much. He can have cookies and cakes on rare occasions, but he has decided to eat them very slowly and enjoy every bite. He even saves some for the next day. Nick has self-control.

1. Why does Nick's mother control the sweets he eats?

a. Sugary food is not healthy.

b. They can't afford to buy more than one dessert a week.

2. What does it mean "on rare occasions"?

a. Every day.

b. Not every day.

3. What is Nick's strategy to eat sweets more often than his mother allows?

a. He doesn't eat all at once but saves them for the next day.

b. He eats what he likes the most.

4. Nick has:

a. Self-confidence

b. Self-control.

5. What is the difference between Chancey and Nick?

a. Chancey does not have self-control.

b. Nick has self-control.

c. a and b are correct.

D. What is the setting? Read the sentences below to identify the time of the day, location, or the season (winter, summer etc.).

1. As night ended, the sunlight splashed across the room.

_____

2. The snow was falling heavily in the valley as the temperature dropped.

_____

3. Oscar made his way to the shore when he saw a shark swimming towards him.

_____

4. I could not see the stars nor the path in front of me, so I turn on my flashlight.

_____

5. It was almost 4 o'clock when the nurse called me to go into the doctor's office.

_____

E. The Microwave (easy).

Percy Spencer was an engineer who worked for a radar company. He always carried a peanut butter candy bar in his pocket to feed it to the squirrels during his lunch break. While working in front of a magnetron, he noticed that the candy bar started to warm up and melt in his pocket. After some experimentation, he invented the microwave.

1. What is the main topic in this paragraph?

_____

2. Who is Percy Spencer?

_____

3. What was his profession?

_____

4. Why did he carry a candy bar in his pocket?

_____

5. What happened to the candy bar while he was working with a magnetron?

_____

F. Main idea

The main idea is what the writer wants us to know about the topic. It is a skill that will be useful for life. The 5 Ws and the How from chapter 14 can help you identify the main idea.

1. Margie enjoys reading fiction books, so she often goes to the library because she reads three books a week.

This is not about the library or how many books she reads weekly.

If she must go to the library often because she reads many books, we are left with two words that describe the main idea: read and enjoy.

Main idea: Margie enjoys reading.

2. Dorothy can't stand to be around dogs, and she doesn't like when they bark. She avoids going to homes where dogs are present.

———

3. The snow began to fall early in the afternoon and didn't stop until the following day. It was challenging to shovel the snow from the sidewalk.

———

4. Crocodiles have large jaws and sharp teeth. They can bite through steel.

———

5. A dinosaur could measure up to 40 metres and weight up to 77.000 Kilograms.

———

6. What is the main idea in this picture?

   a. The children are holding the rackets.

   b. The girl is a better player than the boy.

   c. The children are playing ping-pong.

7. What is the main idea in this picture?

   a. Two cowgirls talking.

   b. The weather is beautiful.

   c. One horse doesn't want to eat.

8. What is the main idea in this picture?

   a. The student is short.

   b. The teacher is explaining something to him.

   c. The teacher's skirt is funny.

9. What is the main idea in this picture?

   a. The lady is shorter than the man.

   b. The man is handsome.

   c. They are in love.

35. Reading Comprehension – Moral Stories

Note to the instructor: The following readings can be challenging to some children because of the text's length. The ability to understand a text is rewarding. It is worth spending extra time, even if this is the only activity of the day. Consider these steps:

a. The person helping with the activity should read the questions first.

b. Read the text out loud to the child and at the same time underline the keywords you find that are clues for the answers.

c. Give the child paper and pencil and start to read three sentences at a time. Give time to the child to draw pictures that match the sentences.

d. Ask the child to tell you, in sequence, the story from the drawings.

e. Let the child read the text out loud.

f. Encourage the child to find the text that is related to the picture.

g. Let the child go back to the text if necessary.

h. Chose three to four questions only based on the child's understanding.

Some children will not need to go through all these steps.

1. The teddy bear.

A young man worked in the lobby of a hotel. One day he heard a little girl crying because she had lost her dear teddy bear. The manager and the chambermaid had already looked for the teddy but did not find it.

The young man said that he would like to help them, so he went to the hotel's laundry room, and after hours of searching for it, found the teddy bear between some bedsheets. He took it to the little girl who, tired of crying and waiting, was asleep on her mother's lap. When she woke up and saw her stuffed friend, she was delighted and thankful. Before leaving the hotel, the mother took a picture of the young man with her daughter and the teddy. She asked permission to use the image, and he agreed.

No one knew, but she owned a chain of toy stores. Upon returning to her office, she made posters out of that picture and placed them in all the stores. The employees were to explain to customers the importance of the image.

The mother decided that she needed extra help, someone who knew the importance of making a child happy. So, she invited the young man to work as a manager in one of her stores.

When he saw the photo taken at the hotel hanging on the store's wall, he was humbled. Written on the picture was a message that read: Making a child happy is priceless

a. Where was the young man working when the little girl lost her teddy?

_____

b. Why was the little girl crying?

_____

c. Had someone tried to help her already? Who?

_____

d. Where did the young man go after he offered to help find the teddy bear?

_____

e. Where did he find her toy?

_____

f. How long did it take him?

_____

g. Why was the little girl sleeping?

_____

h. What was her reaction when he gave her the bear?

_____

i. What did her mom do before leave the hotel?

_____

j. Why did she ask permission to use the photo?

_____

k. Was the mother a rich and successful woman? How do you know?

_____

l. She had two things done with the picture; what were they?

_____

m. Why do you think the employees were supposed to tell customers about the poster?

_____

n. Do you believe the girl's mother would have offered him the job if the young man had not tried to help find the teddy bear?

_____

o. What have you learned from this story?

_____

_____

2. The neighbours (challenging).

Janelle was a single mother who lived in a quiet neighbourhood with her daughter Janette. Their closest neighbour was a couple who had immigrated from another country. The couple had two children. Janelle never tried to get close to their neighbours because she thought they had nothing in common. In fact, she showed indifference towards them.

One day, when the neighbour's children played soccer, the ball fell into Janelle's backyard. One of the kids went to her door and rang the bell to ask for the ball, but she was not kind and said she would keep it so that they would not bother her anymore.

They were upset and told their parents, and they decided that it would be best to buy another ball instead of arguing with the lady. This incident made them realize that Janelle did not like them.

On a rainy night, the family's doorbell rang. It was Janelle's daughter, Janette. She was frightened and said that her mother had fallen and could not get up. She asked if they could help her. The mother and her two kids went immediately to Janelle's house and decided that it was best to call the ambulance.

Upon arriving at the hospital, a nurse took Janelle and Janette to a room. When the doctor came in, they realized that the doctor was their neighbour with whom they never tried to have a relationship. He was kind to them, but they felt awkward and embarrassed. He said that his wife was worried about her and had called him to explain what had happened. She also wanted to know if Janelle would be ok. Janelle apologized for their behaviour and said that there was no excuse for how she and her daughter had treated them.

They learned an important lesson that day. The doctor said that it is never too late to build a friendship and that some friends are closer than family.

a. What does it mean to show indifference towards someone?

_____

b. Why did Janelle and her daughter never make an effort to have a relationship with their neighbours?

_____

c. Why was Janelle unkind to the kid who asked her to retrieve the ball?

_____

d. What was the kid's parent's response?

_____

e. Why did Janette go to the neighbour's house?

_____

f. How did they respond to Janette's request?

_____

g. Who was the doctor that attended to Janelle at the hospital?

_____

h. How did he treat them?

_____

i. What was Janelle's reaction to being treated by her neighbour?

_____

j. Do you have a friend that is closer to you than a family member?

_____

k. What have you learned from this story?

_____

_____

36. Find Two Things In The Text.

1. Lorna and Yasmin heard their father saying that the sound of the rain was thunderous. They went to the window to look at the backyard grass that was rapidly being covered with hail. They pressed their hands to the glass and watched in wonder as hail balls of different sizes fell. They stayed there for so long that the glass became foggy with their breath.

a. Who are Lorna and Yasmin?

_____

b. Why were they looking outside?

_____

2. Last Sunday, Marco and his wife invited their friends Giovanni and his wife Isabella to go to the park for a picnic. They brought delicious food such as fried chicken with potato salad, freshly baked buns, dessert, and iced tea.

a. How many couples met in the park for a picnic?

_____

b. What is Marco's wife name?

_____

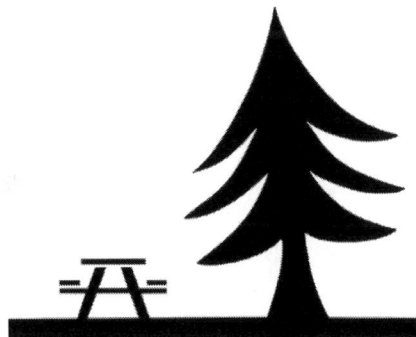

37. Read and Draw.

1. Read the paragraph, paying attention to detail, and then draw the image that the story conveyed with as many details as you can. Pay attention to emotions, facial expressions etc. As you draw, try to pay attention to the *proportion* between objects. For example, a boy opening a big box. Who is more prominent, the boy or the box?

a. Today is Bertha's birthday, and she is *delighted*! She is standing beside a square table with a knife in her hand. The cake is round, covered with yellow icing and red berries. She is wearing a long, pink dress that covers her feet.

b. Bert is a big guy, but he hunches his shoulders when he is standing. Today he is wearing gray pants, a gray shirt, and gray shoes. His posture shows that he is not sure of himself.

c. Molly is holding Bea's right hand. They are both wearing gray pants and blue running shoes. Molly has a yellow long sleeve top on and sunglasses. Bea is wearing a red short-sleeved top and a blue baseball cap.

d. Bob threw his head back, opened his arms and screamed!

e. There were only two students in the classroom with the teacher. All the other desks were empty.

f. The brown dog caught the yellow ball in his mouth.

g. Marcy could see the snow-capped mountains from a distance.

h. The big pink pig is playing in the mud.

i. The girl has a blue flower in her long brown hair.

j. The boy is standing between his big brown dog and his small orange cat.

k. The girl is sitting on the grass watching two birds flying up in the air.

38. Create an Image

Draw a figure out of the lines below, and then write down what it is.

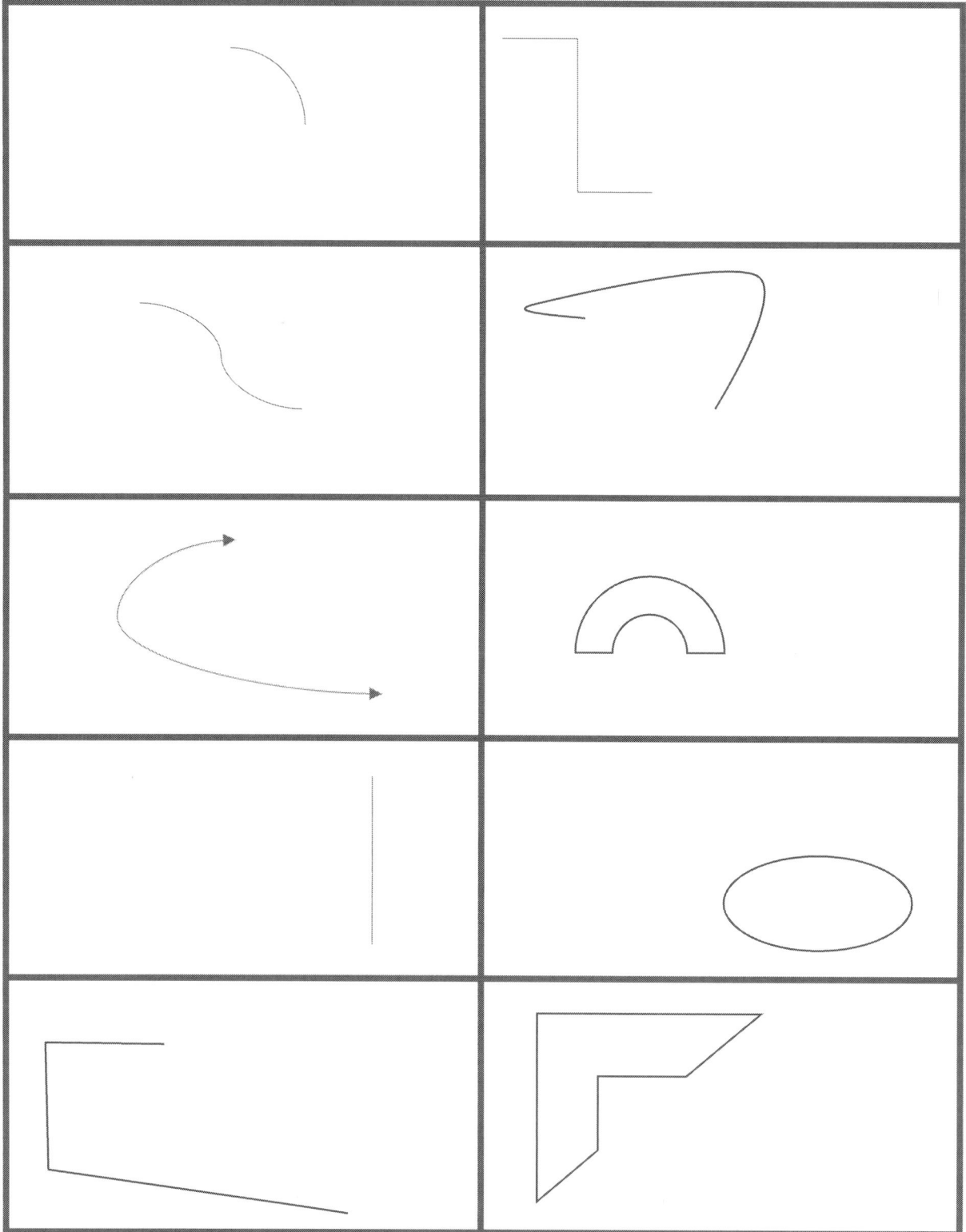

39. Skim and Scan

This technique improves the ability to identify in texts keywords and main ideas through the use of rapid eye movement. Skim and scan through the words bellow and underline the following ones:

1. He   Who   Any   Hers

I, we, you, he, she, it, they, this, these, that, those, who, which, that, as, each, all, everyone, either, one, both, any, such, somebody, who, which, what, myself, herself, mine, yours, his, hers, theirs, my, your, his, her, our, their, I, we, you, he, she, it, they, this, these, that, those, who, which, that, any, each, all, everyone, either, one, both, any, such, somebody, who, which, what, myself, herself, hers, any, such, somebody.

2. Do   Eat   Wash   Dance

Was, were, been, began, begun, do, drive, beat, beaten, become, eat, begun, bent, bet, bid, bite, blow, do, climb, grasp, laugh, paint, eat, feel, find, found, grow, draw.

bring, build, burn, buy, catch, beat, begun, do, drive, eat, feel, find, found, grow, been, beat, beaten, grew, have, ring, drink, run, wash, dance, climb, grasp, laugh, paint, point, part, look, act, chop, sing, dance, call, wash cut, draw, find, give.

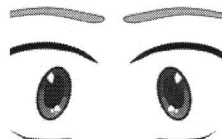

3. About   On   Until   Inside

Aboard, since, about, consider, above, on, versus, across, behind, unlike, concern, below, into, over, past, beneath, unlike, besides, above, inside, except, following, inside, of, plus, round, then, under, for, on, save, to, until, concern, upon, from, towards, per, onto, near, minus, like, inside, above, aboard, on, until, across, behind, unlike, besides, above, inside, near, minus, like, inside, above, below, into, over, past, inside, save, to.

4. O   Our   Thee   Land   We

O Canada! Our home and native land! True patriot love, in all thy sons command.

With glowing hearts we see thee rise, the True North strong and free!

From far and wide, O Canada, we stand on guard for thee. God keep our land glorious and free! O Canada, we stand on guard for thee. O Canada, we stand on guard for thee. (public domain)

5. Mary   Lamb   Against   See   Rule

Mary had a little lamb, little lamb, little lamb. Mary had a little lamb; its fleece was white as snow. And everywhere that Mary went, Mary went, Mary went, everywhere that Mary went, the lamb was sure to go. He followed her to school one day, school one day, school one day. He followed her to school one day, which was against the rule. It made the children laugh and play, laugh and play, laugh and play. It made the children laugh and play to see a lamb at school.

40. Pronoun Reverse

1. Cristina is reading a book. _____ loves to read.

2. My mom asked me to play the piano quietly while ____ was talking on the phone with dad. ____ were talking about ____ family vacation next year.

3. Eva and Lorne are siblings. ____ built a snowman in ____ backyard.

4. Robert doesn't like it when the sun is too hot. ____ prefers cooler temperatures.

5. My mom asked me where my sister Hannah was. ____ told ____ that ____ didn't know where Hannah was.

6. Alys had a great day at school! _____ handed in all _____ homework and spent recess time playing with Bonnie and Allana. ____ are ____ best friends.

7. Elizabeth loves going to the zoo with _____ dad. This trip is something that ____ do every summer since _____ was a little girl.

8. After lunch, Bailey and Horace will go to the gym to play basketball. ____ is ____ favourite sport.!

9. The pet store was filled with customers. ____ were all looking at the beautiful macaw. ____ had very colourful feathers and a long beak.

10. Harry walked carefully through the snow-covered parking lot. _____ was holding a box full of drinking glasses. ____ were a gift for ____ sister's new apartment.

11. The elderly woman could hear the children. ____ were playing in _____ backyard. However, ____ had not invited _____ to play there.

12. My mom drove Jenny, Paul, and me to Max's party.

My mom drove _____ to Max's party.

13. Mary Lou and I went to the mall.

____ went to the mall.

14. Breanna did not mind driving Caleb and M.C. to the river to find the lost canoe.

Breanna did not mind driving _____ to the river to find the canoe that was lost.

15. Gordon bought Lorentz a coffee mug. When Lorentz saw _____, he was delighted.

16. Leticia, Kaylee, and Simone went to the barn to saddle _____ horses.

17. Cinch was not always healthy. As a child, _____ was sickly and fragile.

18. Clancy's parents bought a new ranch. _____ want to raise cattle.

19. Luan started to work out with a friend. _____ went to the gym every day.

20. Sailors need lighthouses to warn _____ of dangerous conditions.

21. Donny has no friends. ____ is a loner.

22. My name is Robert, _____ work for the government.

23. My parents and I live on an island. _____ neighbours are fisherman.

24. Mr. Ould asked all the students in our class to clean the hallway. Some of _____ refused to help.

25. The zookeeper relocated the animals because of the flood. Some of _____ went to zoos in other provinces.

26. I am going to the beach, and _____ need to take sunscreen with _____. I don't know where _____ is, so I will ask _____ neighbour if I can borrow _____.

27. Judah and I are going to Vancouver right now. _____ need to pack _____ bags immediately, otherwise _____ will miss the flight.

28. My mom and my dad are coming to watch me play baseball. _____ are my biggest fans.

29. My friends and I went to watch the Calgary Philharmonic Orchestra. After the concert, _____ went to the Calgary Tower for dinner.

30. Armando forgot to tell Angela and Nathan that _____ was not going out with _____ anymore.

41. Odd One Out

1. Which one of the following is not an aquatic animal?

a. Whales   b. Mollusks   c. Kangaroo rat   d. Jellyfish

2. The following are essential to our bodies, except:

a. Water   b. Chemicals   c. Food   d. Protein

3. The following belong together, except:

a. Shoulder   b. Neck   c. Knee   d. Head

4. When talking about the weather, all but one term is correct:

a. Air   b. Forehead   c. Chinook   d. Blizzard

5. Which of the following is the least accurate about reading?

a. Colour helps increase attention.

b. Bright colour draws attention to the text.

c. All colours are suitable for reading.

6. Which of the following is not true about Alberta?

a. Alberta is a province.

b. Calgary is the capital of Alberta.

c. Banff National Park is in the province of Alberta.

7. Which one of these is not a lake in Canada?

a. Lake Garda   b. Moraine Lake   c. Lake Louise   d. Lake Superior

8. Which one does not belong to the group?

a. Salt   b. Pepper   c. Chili   d. Bread

9. Which one does not belong in the living room?

a. Piano   b. Couch   c. Bed   d. Coffee Table

10. Which one should not be at the dinner table?

a. Chair   b. Glasses   c. Broom   d. Cutlery

11. All of these are tropical fruits, except:

a. Papaya   b. Blueberry   c. Banana   d. Pineapple

12. Which one of the following is not a flower?

a. Tomato   b. Rose   c. Jasmine   d. Orchid

13. All of these objects should be in the classroom, except:

a. Chalk   b. Desks   c. Chairs   d. Toilet

14. Which of these months have the least amount of rain?

a. July   b. January   c. March   d. September

15. Which one of the following is not a winter sport?

a. Beach volleyball   b. Snowboarding

c. Bobsled   d. Ice skating

16. All of the following facts are true about Canada, except:

a. Canada is in North America

b. Canada is the second-largest country in the world.

c. The capital of Canada is Ottawa.

d. Canada has only one type of climate condition.

17. Emily has three dogs and two cats. They are all brown, but one of the dogs has white spots on its back. His name is Spot.

- Which one of the following sentences is not true?

a. Emily has five animals in total.

b. Emily has more dogs than cats.

c. One of Emily's cats has spots on its fur.

d. All her animals are brown.

18. Mulan lives in Budapest, Hungary with her parents and her two brothers. Their house is simple but extremely comfortable. However, the boys tell their school friends that they live in big house, in a prestigious area of the city.

- This paragraph explains all of the followings, except:

a. Mulan has two brothers.

b. They live in a simple but comfortable home.

c. The boys are ashamed of their house.

d. The house is near their school.

19. All these shapes have something in common, except:

a. Circle   b. Square   c. Triangle   d. Rectangle

20. These holidays are celebrated only in Canada, except:

a. Canada Day   b. Victoria Day

c. Family Day   d. Independence Day

21. The cat, the spider and the kangaroo decided to go for a walk, but the weather forecast said it would rain. The kangaroo asked the umbrella if she wanted to go out with them, and she said, yes.

- Of all the characters that went outside, which one is not a living creature?

a. Cat   b. Spider   c. Kangaroo   d. Umbrella

22. Jon removed the ball from the bag and put his helmet, mouthguard, and gloves in it.

- Which one of these items is not hockey equipment?

a. Ball   b. Helmet   c. Mouthguard   d. Gloves

23. I could see the ocean from my window as the train made its way up the mountain. There was a flash of lightning, and soon, a loud clap of thunder.

- Which one of the following does not create sound.

a. Ocean   b. Window   c. Lightning   d. Thunder

24. Trina set the table for the party with delicious food that included cake, pie, muffins and cantaloupe. Identify the food that contains the least amount of sugar:

a. Cake   b. Cantaloupe   c. Muffins   d. Pie

25. You can ski in all these countries, except:

a. Norway   b. Italy   c. Brazil   d. France

26. Banff, Jasper, Waterton, and Crimson Lake are parks in the province of Alberta. Which one is not a National Park?

a. Banff   b. Jasper   c. Waterton   d. Crimson Lake

27. Polar bears cannot go to jail anywhere in the world, except in:

a. Russia   b. Greenland   c. Canada   d. Norway

28. The aurora borealis lights up the sky in all these countries, except in:

a. Finland   b. Japan   c. Sweden   d. Canada

29. Which one of the following statements is not right about the moon?

a. The moon orbits the earth.

b. The moon is inhabited.

c. The moon is full of craters.

30. Canada is not known for:

a. Maple Syrup   b. Statue of Liberty

c. Hockey   d. Cold winter

42. What Is That Sound?

Note to the educator: Choose a song that is appropriate for the student's level of understanding. Let the student listen to it once, then play it again. On the second time, ask students to answer the following questions. Repeat this exercise frequently.

Note to Students: After listening to the music, answer the following questions:

1. What instrument or instruments do you hear? (add instruments if necessary)

a. Piano   b. Acoustic Guitar c. Electrical Guitar

d. Drums   e. Voice   f. Violin   g. Bass Guitar   h. Organ

2. Is the song played by a/an:

a. Band   b. Orchestra   c. Solo Artist

3. Who is singing?

a. Solo Artist   b. Choir   c. Three to Eight Vocalists

4. What is the musical genre?

a. Pop Music   b. Country Music c. Rock & Roll   d. Opera

e. Hip Hop   f. Rap   g. Techno   h. Jazz

5. The tempo is:

a. Slow   b. Medium   c. Fast

6. Do you know the name of this song and the artist? If not, search for it online by writing some of the lyrics on the search bar, if available.

43. Put It In Order

1. Rearrange your daily routine according to your schedule.

You can create a list that applies to your schedule.

a. Go to School

b. Take a Shower

c. Go to Sleep

d. Eat Supper

e. Eat Breakfast

f. Table Work (Homework)

g. Eat Lunch

h. Do Chores at Home

i. Extra-Curricular Activities

j. Wake Up

k. Have a Break

l. Watch TV

m. Play

n. Spend Time with Family

o. Make my bed

p. Snack Time

_____

_____

_____

_____

_____

_____

_____

_____

_____

_____

_____

_____

_____

_____

_____

_____

44. Fill In The Blanks

A. Fill in the blanks with the correct answer:

1. Tell me _____ what you are thinking.

a. Of   b. About   c. Some

2. The boy went to the store to buy _____ apples.

a. Of   b. About   c. Some

3. Mark claimed _____ he was too tired to do his homework.

a. Of   b. About   c. That

4. He should _____ passed his driving test.

a. Of   b. Have   c. Some

5. David told me _____ the time he went to Israel.

a. Of   b. About   c. With

6. He was innocent _____ the crime.

a. Of   b. With   c. About

7. We all suspected him _____ cheating.

a. Of   b. About   c. With

8. My answer _____ your question is in the envelope.

a. About   b. To   c. Of

9. This place is _____ exhibition and shows.

a. Of   b. About   c. For

10. I put a note on the door _____ privacy.

a. Of   b. For   c. About

11. I feel deeply sorry _____ your loss.

a. Of   b. With   c. For

12. People _____ a lot of money are not always happy.

a. Of   b. With   c. For

13. I prefer to read _____ the library.

a. With   b. Of   c. At

14. Please put the vase _____ table.

a. On   b. Of   c. At

15. I am excited to move _____ Ireland.

a. To   b. Of   c. At

16. Prince Edward Island is famous _____ Anne of Green Gables.

a. With   b. Of   c. For

17. She insisted _____ paying for the meal.

a. On   b. Of   c. At

18. Please, stop laughing _____ me.

a. With   b. Of   c. At

19. I am bored _____ my job.

a. With   b. Of   c. At

B. Fill in the blanks in these conditional sentences:

1. I do not think she is worried about us. *If* she were, *she would* have phoned us.

2. _____ you heat the water to 100 C, it boils.

3. _____ we don't leave this moment; we will miss the train.

4. _____ I had known that you were coming, I _____ have baked a cake.

5. You could have gone with us, _____ we had known you were in town.

6. I _____ have gone to Japan with you _____ I had extra money.

7. _____ she is late, we _____ go without her.

8. _____ Joanne had not studied, she _____ have failed the test.

9. _____ I didn't work extra hours, I _____ be able to pay my bills.

10. _____ you don't work hard, you _____ be promoted.

C. This activity has two steps. First, fill in the blanks below and then write a short story using those words.

Example of Action verb: run, kick, eat. Example of Adjectives: delicious, bumpy, noisy.

Name of a town or a city: _____

Name of a family member: _____

Time of day: _____

Action verb: _____

Type of flower: _____

A thing: _____

A place: _____

A colour: _____

A day of the week or the month: _____

Adjective: _____

A type of feeling: _____

A Month: _____

D. Now come up with a title and write the short story with the words you wrote above.

_____

_____

_____

_____

45. Where Would You Go?

1. Where would you go downhill skiing?

a. Your backyard.

b. Nakiska.

c. Serengeti.

2. Where would you go tobogganing?

a. Crimson Lake, AB.

b. A hill.

c. At the tennis court.

3. Where would you go surfing?

a. The Atlantic Ocean.

b. Banff.

c. Swimming pool.

4. Where would you go cross-country skiing?

a. Great Wall of China.

b. Sahara Desert.

c. Lake Louise.

5. Where would you go to see a collection of artifacts with cultural and historical importance?

 a. Library.

b. Museum.

c. Hotel.

6. Where would you go to see wild animals roaming free?

a. Zoo.

b. Animal Sanctuary.

c. Safari.

7. Where would you go to see a rocket launch?

a. Rocky Mountains.

b. Old Harry Rocks.

c. NASA, Cape Canaveral, Florida.

8. Where would you go to see the Statue of Liberty?

a. New York City.

b. Liberty City.

c. Liberty University.

46. Follow Directions

1. *Read* the instructions *first* and then *write* the answers on the corresponding *lines below.*

   a. Use a pencil to write the number of days that are in September.

   b. Use a black pen to write the months of the year that have 30 days.

   c. Use a red pen to write the month of the year that has the least number of days.

   d. Use a brown crayon to write the month of the year in which spring starts.

a. _____

b. _____

c. _____

d. _____

2. Archeology

a. If it is Monday, write the word "dinosaur" in yellow. If not, write it in purple.

b. Before you write the word "archeologist" in black, write the word "shovel" in blue.

c. Draw three eggs side by side. The first one is orange; the second one is gray, the third one is red.

d. Circle, the word "shovel" from answer "b" with a brow pencil, then write the word "finished."

a. _____

b. _____

c. _____

d. _____

3. Technology

a. Write the brand name of your mother's cell phone using a pencil.

b. If there is a laptop in your house, write the word "laptop" with a red pen and in capital letters. If there is a desktop computer in your home, write the word "desktop" with a red pen and small caps. If you have both, write the word "both" with a blue pen and capitalize the first letter.

c. Before writing the word "technology" with a purple pencil, write the word "digital" with a blue pen.

d. Underline the cell phone's brand name in answer "a" with a yellow pencil, and then write the word "horse" with a gray pencil.

a. _____

b. _____

c. _____

d. _____

4. Colours.

a. Write the word "black" using a red pen and the word "white" using a black pen.

b. Write the word "yellow" using a green pencil and the word "green" using a blue pencil.

c. Write the word "blue" using a red pencil and the word "red" using a yellow pencil.

d. Say the <u>colour of each word</u> out loud as fast as you can (if blue is written in yellow, say "yellow"). Then, write down whether that exercise was easy or difficult.

a. _____

b. _____

c. _____

d. _____

Create your own "follow instruction" game and then ask someone to play with you.

5. You need a separate page with lines and margins to do this activity. *(Challenging)*

a. Write your first name on the top right-hand corner of the page.

b. In the left margin, starting on the second line, write the numbers 1 to 10, one under the other.

c. Beside number 3, draw three hearts.

d. Colour the middle heart red.

e. Beside every even number, draw a blue smiley face.

f. Write your last name at the bottom left-hand corner of the page.

g. Go to the washroom, wash your hands, and read the next instruction.

h. Go to the kitchen, leave your watch (or any object) on the table. Return for the next instruction.

i. Circle number 10 in question number b.

j. Go back to instruction "e" and colour the first heart yellow.

k. Go to the kitchen and get your watch. Return for the next instruction.

l. On the next line, write the letter of the alphabet that comes right after the direction you are reading now. Then say aloud: Done!

47. Creative Writing

1. Read the text below and then use your creativity and research to fill in the blanks. Pay attention to context (parts of something written that form an idea),

Many towns in Canada _____. I am always amazed by the fact that many people don't _____

_____. People from all over the world come to Canada to visit places like Lake Louise. However, _____.

In Alberta, for instance, there are towns such as Marketville. This town was founded in _____. Soon after, they opened a cheese factory, _____. At first, they struggled to keep things going, but with the help of Dr. Marker, _____. Up to that time, the town was called _____, but in appreciation to Dr. Marker's involvement, _____. Today, Marketville has a population of _____, but the creamery is _____, which attracts people from many places to learn about its history.

2. Three things.

A. Write three things you could use a vehicle for other than driving:

1. _____

2. _____

3. _____

B. Write three things you can do at a lake other than swimming:

1._____

2._____

3._____

C. Write three things you could use a broom for other than sweeping:

1._____

2._____

3._____

D. Write three things you could use tennis balls for besides playing tennis.

1._____

2._____

3._____

E. Write three things you can do with a toothbrush other than brushing teeth:

1._____

2._____

3._____

F. Write three things you can do with socks besides wearing them:

1._____

2._____

3._____

G. Write three things glass jars are used for other than preserving food:

1._____

2._____

3._____

3. Write a short story from the image:

_____
_____
_____
_____
_____
_____
_____
_____
_____
_____
_____
_____
_____

4. Add details to the sentences.

a. I want to go to Tim Hortons.

(why do you want to go to Tim Hortons and what will happened there?).

_____

_____

b. Once there was a doctor who enjoyed helping people.

(where was he and what kind of people?).

_____

_____

c. The hurricane blew the roof of the house.

(what happened to the family?).

_____

_____

d. Celine's school is closed, and bus has been cancelled following a snowfall warning.

(what did she do instead?).

_____

_____

e. My uncle is visiting next week from Namibia.

(why is he coming, and what will he do?).

_____

_____

f. Mimi baked a cake with gluten free flour.

(what was the occasion and why did she use gluten free flour?).

_____

_____

g. Andre flew from Fredericton to Vancouver.

(why did he go to Vancouver and who was with him?).

_____

_____

h. The loud footsteps told us he was here.

(who is he and who is us?).

_____

_____

i. Julie was lost, but she was not afraid.

(who is Julie and why she was not afraid?).

_____

_____

48. Creative Thinking – Use your imagination to answer these questions. There is no wrong answer.

1. How do you think pyjamas got their name?

_____

_____

2. Would animals enjoy wearing glasses? Why or why not?

_____

_____

3. How would you convince a child to make his or her bed?

_____

_____

4. What will cars look like in 50 years?

_____

_____

5. If there were no plates, how would we eat?

_____

_____

6. What kind of conversation would you have with a butterfly?

_____

_____

7. Should a pet wear a seatbelt while driving in a car? Why or why not?

_____

_____

8. What might make a grandparent sad? Why?

_____

_____

9. If pigs could drive, what would be the model of the car? Draw it.

_____

_____

10. If the swings in the park could talk, what would they say?

_____

_____

11. If you were to build a playground only for cats, what equipment would you place in it?

_____

_____

Draw a cat's playground the way you would build it.

49. Multipurpose

Multipurpose is a word used to describe things that we can use in different ways. Find out what the *uses and purposes* of the terms listed below are. You can ask someone, search online, or both.

1. E.g., What is the purpose of water?

 Animals and humans use water for drinking, washing, and regulating body temperature. Aquatic animals depend on water to survive. We can have fun with water when we swim, go canoeing, boating, diving. Water can also be dangerous.

2. Computer.

_____

3. Vehicle.

_____

3. Food.

_____

4. Chair.

_____

5. Paper.

_____

6. Building.

_____

7. Sportplex.

_____

8. Ice ring.

_____

9. Lake.

_____

10. Pillow.

_____

11. Paper Towel.

_____

12. Shampoo.

_____

13. Safety pins.

_____

14. Scarf.

_____

15. Honey.

_____

16. Cotton.

_____

17. Empty spray bottles.

_____

18. Metal box.

_____

19. Garbage bag.

_____

20. Adhesive tapes.

_____

50. Skills:

1. Skill is the ability to do something. Some skills are transferable, meaning that we can use them in different areas of life. Do online research, ask someone about the following skills and write down how someone can use them.

a. Reading: _reading by myself, to someone, at a place of worship, or in school._

b. Speaking: _____

c. Spelling: _____

d. Writing: _____

e. Organizing: _____

f. Patience: _____

g. Adaptability: _____

h. Listening: _____

I. Brainstorm: _____

j. Problem solving: _____

51. First Aid and Emergencies.

A. Safety.

To be safe means to be protected from harm and to be prepared for emergencies. An emergency is a serious situation that happens when we do not expect it, and it requires immediate attention. Examples of emergencies can be a house fire, heavy rains, earthquake, illness, injury, and accidents.

It is vital to know how to proceed in case of a fire at home or elsewhere, but we should also know how to help injured people.

First responders are people trained to aid during an emergency. They would include the police, firefighters, and paramedics. There are many reasons why everyone should know basic safety and first aid. This knowledge can prevent an emergency from getting worse and even save lives. Simple things like knowing when to call 911 or stop a nosebleed can make a lot of difference.

1. What does it mean to be safe?

_____

_____

2. What is an emergency?

_____

_____

3. Do you know what to do in case of a fire at home and away from home?

_____

_____

4. Who are the first responders?

_____

_____

5. How can we help in case of an emergency?

_____

_____

B. Fire.

Individuals with special needs must have a support network of people who understand their needs. Some individuals use a writing app to keep facts about their disabilities for emergencies. You might want to consider this option.

Have a fire drill at home so everyone will know what to do in case of fire. Remind your parents to change the batteries in the fire alarm. Everyone should know what the best escape route is out of the house and where to meet outside. Find out where the locks and screens are on the windows and learn how to open them. If your bedroom is on the second floor, you might need to buy a collapsible ladder to help with your escape.

Don't forget your pets. Get out of the house first, and then call 911.

Watch this video with your family:

Keywords for search engine: Toronto.ca home fire escape.

https://www.toronto.ca/community-people/public-safety-alerts/safety-tips-prevention/home-high-rise-school-workplace-safety/home-fire-escape-planning/

1. Do you have a list of the things you need, such as medication? If not, write one.

_____

_____

_____

2. Do you know what the best escape route is out of your house?

_____

_____

3. After watching the video, do you know how many minutes you might have to leave a house that is on fire?

_____

_____

4. When should you call 911?

_____

_____

When to call 911 – Only in case of emergency.

C. **911**

You may call 911 at any time of the day or the night, but only when people are in danger or are seriously injured. If you know a person with an underlying health problem, you should know the symptoms that would require you to call 911.

When you call 911, the person who answers will ask what the emergency is and if they need to contact police, the fire department or an ambulance. At this time, you should explain your situation and what is happening. *Remember words such as fire, injury, fall, and bleeding.*

D. **First Aid Kit**.

A **basic first aid kit** should include:

Adhesive tape	Gauze	Instant cold and hot packs	Cotton balls
Cotton swabs	Disposable gloves	Petroleum jelly	Tweezers
Hand sanitizer	Antibiotic ointment	Hydrogen peroxide	

1. Cold and hot compress.

* Use a hot compress to relax and soothe sore muscles.

* Use cold compress in injuries, such as swelling and bruises.

2. Stop heavy bleeding.

* Put pressure on the cut with a clean cloth and remove when the bleeding stops.

3. Nosebleed.

* Sit straight up and pinch the nose shut and breathe through your mouth.

4. Minor cuts.

* Clean the area with water or antiseptic spray and cover with an adhesive bandage or Band-Aid.

Answer the following questions:

1. Fleur fell from her bike and scraped her knee. Should you call 911?

a. Yes   b. No

2. How would you treat Fleur's knee?

3. If someone hits their elbow and it swells, what kind of compress would you use?

a. cold   b. hot

4. Denzel fell down the stairs and is unconscious. Should you call 911?

a. Yes   b. No

5. What is your home address?

_____

_____

6. What is the best phone number to reach you?

_____

7. Do you have an emergency contact person? What is their phone number?

_____

8. What is Mom and Dad's real names?

_____

9. There are numerous reasons why people should have basic first aid knowledge—list two of them.

_____

_____

10. Do you have a first aid kit in your home? If so, do you know where it is?

_____

_____

52. Sexual Harassment.

Sexual harassment is a form of bullying and harassment. For example, it can be a comment that makes a person feel bad or an unwanted touch, but neither is okay.

You should feel free to talk to your family or friends if you think someone is harassing you. Many times, harassment happens among people that know each other. You should always make clear to the person who is harassing you that their action is unwanted. In Canada, harassment and discrimination are illegal. Examples of sexual harassment behaviour:

- o Teasing someone about their gender or physical appearance.
- o Asking for physical touch or sexual touch that is unwanted.
- o Making comments and jokes about private activities and private body parts.
- o Starring too much at someone's body or clothes.
- o Showing videos or images with sexual content to someone who doesn't want to see it.
- o Unwanted or unwelcome touching, patting or pinching.
- o Rubbing against another person's body.
- o Asking for unwanted sexual favours such as touching another person in a private part on their body
- o Contacting, demanding, and threatening a person that does not want contact.
- o Physically assaulting someone.

Your body is your own, and no one has the right to talk about it or touch it in any way that makes you uncomfortable. Ask for help if any of these things happen.

1. Sexual harassment is unwelcome sexual advances, requests for sexual favours, and other verbal or physical conduct of a sexual nature.

a. True   b. False

2. I should talk to a family member or a trusted friend if I feel harassed.

a. True   b. False

3. Sometimes, a family member or an acquaintance can harass me.

a. True   b. False

4. We can say things like, "move away from me," "stop touching me," "don't say that again," or "I don't want to see this" to a person that is making us uncomfortable.

a. True   b. False

5. Sexual harassment is a form of discrimination.

a. True   b. False

6. Sending unrequested nude images and videos by email and text is a form of sexual harassment.

a. True   b. False

7. A hug between friends is not considered harassment.

a. True   b. False

53. Good Manners.

Good manners are important because it *makes our social life more pleasant and peaceful.*

Bad manners can *keep us from being invited* to places and occasions that might be important to us.

These skills are good for our *self-esteem* because it makes us *feel good on the inside.* It is good to remember that *sometimes* we have to *go out of our way* to show that we care. For example, some people suffer from a condition called *misophonia*, which means *"hatred of sound."* Those who have misophonia *react negatively* to the *sound* of people chewing with their mouth open, slurping on beverages and soups, and other ordinary human sounds. Good manners require that we respect people with this condition.

1. Good manners means:

a. To treat people with courtesy, showing good social behaviour.

b. Treat people with disrespect and rudeness.

2. When we use good manners around people, we show:

a. Disrespect   b. Respect

3. When a person is speaking to you:

a. Make eye contact and listen   b. Look at your cell phone.

4. During meals at home or a restaurant, you should:

a. Start eating before everybody else   b. Wait until everyone starts eating

5. What should you do if you burp, especially in front of strangers?

a. Say, "excuse me"   b. Don't say anything

6. It is *never* polite to talk with your mouth full.

a. True   b. False

7. There are people from all over the world living in Canada, and table manners are different from country to country. When people are eating out or have guests over:

a. They should not speak with their mouth full, nor slurp on drinks.

b. They should eat however they want.

8. Let's pretend that a person from a culture where chewing loud is acceptable dines with a person from a culture where chewing loud is not considered polite. Keeping in mind that chewing food or bubble-gum loudly can make other people uncomfortable while chewing quietly does not offend anyone, what do you think should happen for the sake of good manners? Explain why.

_____

_____

_____

_____

9. What do you think *could* happen if some friends are *enjoying a meal together,* and one person eats and talks with the mouth full, burps, and slurps the drink?

a. Most people could feel disgusted by the noise.

b. The mealtime could become unpleasant.

b. Some people might look down at the person making the noise.

c. All the answers are correct.

10. Saying "please" and "thank you" is the polite thing to do.

a. True   b. False

11. Older people feel special when we respect them, listen to them, and help them do things they can't do anymore.

a. True   b. False

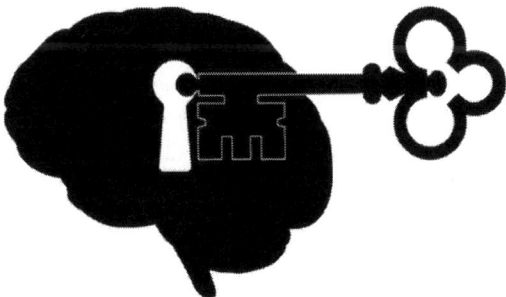

54. Executive Functioning Activities.

We all need executive function abilities to accomplish daily tasks. It can be a simple task like managing our time or as complex as piloting an airplane. These skills allow us to function safely and productively. There are simple activities that we do at home and at school that will help develop these skills.

1. From the list below, check what you can do at home with the help of a parent/sibling or aid.

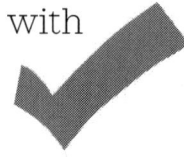

a. Plan a meal: Decide together what the dinner will be. Check for ingredients in the pantry to make sure you have everything. Help to set the table and clean up.

_____

b. Tidy up a room: It does not have to be your bedroom. With help and guidance, look around the house and notice what is out of place, if the floor is dirty, or if you need to put toilet paper in the washroom. Help as much as you can.

_____

c. Think about things that you are struggling with now. Talk to someone, ask for help, brainstorm and prioritize.

_____

d. Think about a movie that you have watched or a book that you have read. What would you change about it? Is there anything that you didn't like? If so, how would you have written that story?

_____

_____

_____

_____

_____

e. Watch a show on TV. Notice the time that you started and write it down. When the show is over, check the time and find out how long the program was.

_____

f. Every morning, when you wake up, look at the time and write it down (or memorize it). When you are ready to go to school, recheck the time to learn how long it took you to get prepared. Is there room for improvement? Should you try to go a little faster the next day?

_____

g. In the morning, ask someone who lives in the same house as you what they want you to remember by at the end of the day. It can be a task, a story, a book's name, a family memory etc. At supper time, repeat to the person what he or she told you in the morning.

_____

h. Plan to learn a new task. Talk to a family member about what would be a great thing to know. This activity is called metacognition.

_____

i. Make a list of all the things you can do by yourself and a list of things you need help to accomplish. Brainstorm and talk to an adult to determine how you can step up and start doing these tasks yourself. There is no need for a prize because being independent is a prize.

_____

j. Practice problem-solving activities. There are many activities online to help you develop this skill. Learn when to ask for help. Be open to learn new things such as how to ask for something, how to play, share, say please and thank you and to know when to ignore a situation or person.

a. What is the problem? _____

_____

b. What are my options? 1. _____

　　　　　　　　　　　　　2. _____

　　　　　　　　　　　　　3. _____

c. Choose the best option. _____

d. Implement the solution. _____

e. Evaluate the results. _____

f. What have you learned from it? _____

55. Types of Decisions.

Should I buy a bike or have a family?

Decision-making is a skill that we use in all areas of our life. As we make the right decisions, we become more confident, independent, and mature. We should learn from our mistakes and, in doing so, improve our ability to make good choices. Read and consider your options before choosing an answer.

1. Which decision is an example of an everyday choice that people might make?

a. Which college to attend.

b. Which types of vehicle to buy.

c. What to eat for dessert.

2. Which decision would have an impact on your adult life?

a. Which T-shirt you should wear.

b. Which career you should choose.

c. Which video game you should play.

3. What is one of the things we should do before making a decision?

a. Do some research.

b. Trust your gut instinct.

c. Make the decision as quick as possible.

4. You have a busy day ahead. What should you do to accomplish your activities?

a. Go with the flow and try to do as much as you can.

b. Make a list of what you need to do and prioritize.

5. What decision can impact you financially?

a. Which movie you will watch.

b. Which vehicle to buy.

56. Would you rather?

A. For Fun.

1. Would you rather have grass or flowers for hair? Why?

_____

_____

2. Would you rather smell like onions or garlic? Why?

_____

_____

3. Would you rather have a giraffe's neck or an elephant's trunk? Why?

_____

_____

4. Would you rather have an octopus' arms or a caterpillar's leg? Why?

_____

_____

5. Would you rather live without electricity or plumbing? Why?

_____

_____

6. Would you rather be able to fly or read minds? Why?

_____

_____

7. Would you rather have a wolf with a cat head or a cat with a wolf's head? Why?

_____

_____

8. Would you rather meet Santa or the Easter Bunny? Why?

_____

_____

9. Would you rather jump into a pool filled with frozen chocolate or frozen strawberries? Why?

_____

_____

B. Serious but fun.

1. Would you rather be a pro sports player or a professional chef? Why?

_____

_____

2. Would you rather be a famous race car driver or a famous singer? Why?

_____

_____

3. Would you rather take music lessons or pottery lessons? Why?

_____

_____

4. Would you rather be a police officer or a fireman? Why?

_____

_____

5. Would you rather be a mountain climber or a skydiver? Why?

_____

_____

6. Would you rather live in the country or the city? Why?

_____

_____

7. Would you rather donate a big prize or receive one? Why?

_____

_____

8. Would you rather be an archeologist or an astronaut? Why?

_____

_____

9. Would you rather be a teacher or a detective? Why?

_____

_____

10. Do you have a favourite "would you rather" question? What is it?

_____

_____

57. Online Search

A. Use your favourite search engine to find answers to these questions:

1. Water boils at what temperature?

Celsius _____   Fahrenheit _____

2. Name 3 of the most famous plays by William Shakespeare.

_____

_____

3. Name five countries that begin with the letter A.

_____

_____

4. List four countries that speak Portuguese.

_____

_____

5. The statue of Christ the Redeemer is in what country?

_____

6. Where is the Taj Mahal Located?

_____

7. Name three animals that lay eggs.

_____

8. Name one popular movie by Chris Hemsworth.

_____

9. Who wrote The Lion, the Witch and the Wardrobe?

_____

10. What would you need to know to make toys?

_____

_____

11. How did the idea of a rubber duckie in the bath first begin?

_____

_____

12. How many squares are there on a checkerboard?

_____

13. What is Mickey Mouse's dog's name?

_____

14. What kind of animal is Babar?

_____

15. What is the capital of New York state?

_____

16. What do frogs have in their mouth that toads do not?

_____

17. What country borders Spain?

_____

18. Who wrote "The Cat and the Hat"?

_____

19. How many queen bees are in each hive?

_____

20. Who was the first Prime Minister of Israel?

_____

21. Who is the 'friendly ghost" of the animated cartoon series?

_____

22. Name the Great Lakes.

_____

23. Who painted the Mona Lisa?

_____

24. What substance inside the corn makes it pop?

_____

25. How many sides are there in a snowflake?

_____

26. How many wings does a bee have?

_____

B. Your favourite movie.

Go online and watch one or two trailers of a famous movie and then answer the following questions. Repeat this exercise with other films and watch it as many times as is necessary. This is an excellent exercise to do before going to the movie theatre.

1. Is the movie based on a book or comic? If so, who is the author (s)?

_____

_____

2. What is the name of the leading actor? (The person who plays the primary role in the movie). If this is an animated movie, which actor does the voice-over?

_____

_____

3. What is the name of the main character?

_____

_____

4. What is the plot? (The events that make up a story – what it is about)

_____

_____

5. Does the movie have a villain? If so, what is the actor's name?

_____

6. What is the name of the villain?

_____

7. What is your favourite thing about the movie?

_____

_____

8. What do you like the most about the main character?

_____

_____

58. How Many Answers?

1. How many answers can you come up with for each of these questions?

a. "Be sure not to lose these," said Sammi as she and her friend left for a camping trip.

What are "these"?

_____

_____

_____

b. How would you know that your neighbour is having guests over for dinner?

_____

_____

_____

c. How can you tell if a person is physically strong?

_____

_____

_____

d. How can you know that it is windy without going outside?

_____

_____

_____

e. "I don't want anymore," said Joe as he handed the plate back to his mom. What could it be that he does not want?

_____

_____

_____

f. How can you know that a person worked outdoors on a hot day?

_____

_____

_____

g. How to make orange juice?

_____

_____

_____

59. Word Play

1. Imagine you live in a world where there are only twenty words. These words are essential for everyday living. Which ones would they be?

1. _____	11. _____
2. _____	12. _____
3. _____	13. _____
4. _____	14. _____
5. _____	15. _____
6. _____	16. _____
7. _____	17. _____
8. _____	18. _____
9. _____	19. _____
10. _____	20. _____

2. Write a paragraph or a sentence with some of these words.

_____

_____

_____

_____

_____

60. Colour Play

1. Name the colours of the following words. If the word *blue* is written in *plum,* you will say *plum.*

Blue	Brown	Red	Beige
Green	Pink	Purple	Orange
Yellow	Black	Gray	Plum

2. Chose a song that you like, and then use the colours green, blue and orange to write the lyrics on the lines.

_____

_____

_____

_____

3. These two men seem to be arguing. Colour them, choose a name for each one, and write about their argument.

_____

_____

_____

_____

4. Colour this image and write the name of the song he is singing+-.

_____

_____

_____

_____

_____

5. Colour the gift box and then write what is in it and the name of the person who will receive it.

_____

_____

_____

_____

6. Colour the house and then write about the people who live there.

_____

_____

_____

_____

_____

7.

8.

10.

11.

_____

_____

Answer Key

1. All About You – page 7

1 to 5: Answers will vary.

6. What Does It Look Like? – page 23

1. b and c 2. a and c 3. a and b 4. a and c

5. a and b 6. a and b 7. a and b 8. a and c

7. Problem Solving – page 25

A. 1. a. The coordinator cancelled the trip to the

mountains because of the weather.

b. Answers will vary.

E.g. Not get upset and talk to the coordinator.

2. a. The people sitting in front of me at the movie

theatre did not stop talking.

b. Answers will vary.

E.g. Politely asked them to keep their voices down.

3. a. Someone was sitting on my favourite bench

during lunch recess.

b. Answers will vary.

E.g. I will not get upset and find another

place to sit down.

4. a. There were no kids at the party I went

with my parents.

b. Answers will vary.

E.g. I asked for a book or a game to keep me

occupied.

5. a. My friends served food that I don't like.

b. Answers will vary.

E.g. I will say thank you and eat some of the side

dishes.

6. a. At the birthday party, the kids only play

board games, which I don't like.

b. Answers will vary.

E.g. I will play for a while with them.

B. a. Problem: John did not know what he should

take to school for show and tell.

Solution: He asked his mom for an idea

b. Problem: Emily had to be at school earlier, but

her mom was out of town.

Solution: She left the house earlier and walked to

school.

c. Problem: Mrs. Anderson did not find pineapple at

the grocery store near her house.

Solution: She went to another store.

d. Problem: Robert saw the rising floodwater.

Solution: He saddled his horse and moved the cattle

to a higher land.

food that I don't like.

b. Answers will vary.

8. What Would You do? – page 28

a. Answers will vary.

E.g. If they are of the same flavour, pour all the

soda

in a jug and serve it in cups

9. Emotions and Affection – page 29

1. a,b, and c 2. c. 3. c.

4. Answers will vary.

E.g. By how they treat me.

5. Answers will vary.

E.g. Offer assistance

6. Answers will vary.

E.g. Recycling.

7. Answers will vary.

E.g. Exercise, read, and laugh

8. Answers will vary.

10. Facts Vs. Opinion – page 31

1. a. Fact b. Opinion c. Fact d. Opinion

e. Opinion f. Opinion g. Fact h. Opinion

i. Fact j. Opinion k. Fact l. Opinion

m. Opinion o. Opinion o. Opinion

p. Fact q. Opinion r. Fact s. Opinion

t. Opinion u. Fact v. Opinion w. Opinion

2. 1. Opinion 2. Facts 3. Opinions

4. Facts 5. Facts 6.Opinions

7. Facts 8. Facts 9. Opinions

10. Facts 11. Opinions 12. Facts

13. Opinions 14. Facts 15. Opinions

3. 1. F O 2. F O 3. F O 4. F O

5. O F 6. F O 7. F O 8. O F 9. F O

10. F O 11. F O 12. F O 13. O F 14. F O

15. O F 16. F O 17. F O 18. O F 19. O F

20. F O 21. F O 22. O F 23. F O

4.

1. These are opinions about the seasons.

2. These are facts about the year.

3. These are pinions about colours

4. These are facts about directions

5. These are opinions about food

6. These are facts about the movie Inkheart

7. These are facts about the sun

5. 1. F O F 2. O O F 3. O O F

4. O F F 5. O O F 6. F F O 7. F F O

6. Answers will vary.

1. F. There are 12 months in a year

O. I wish there were 13 months in a year.

2. F. ____

o. My family is the best in the world.

3. F. ____

O. My city is beautiful

4. F.____

O. I have the best friend in the world.

5. F. Music is composed and performed for many purposes.

O. I cannot live without music.

6. F. Dogs are mammals.

O. Dogs make the best pets.

7. F.____

O. My school is too noisy.

8. F. Skiing is a winter sport.

O.__

9. F. Hockey is a sport played on ice.

O.__

10. F. Cheetah is the fastest land animal on earth.

O. __

11. F. Canada is the second-largest country in the world.

O.__

12. F. Friendship is a relationship of mutual affection between peoples.

O. ___

7. a. F. A castle is a large building

O. __

b. F. Butterflies rely on their feet to taste the food they eat.

O. __

c. F. A car is a wheeled motor vehicle.

O. __

d. F. Logie Baird transmitted the first television picture.

O. __

e. F. A cell phone is a portable telephone.

O.___

f. F. A soccer ball has 32 panels.

O. ___

g. F. Some hockey sticks are made with wood from the maple tree.

O. __

8. Answers will vary.

11. Cause and Effect – page 45

1. a. Cause: To withdraw money

Effect: I went to the bank

b. Cause: To return the movie that I borrowed from her.

Effect: I went to Erika's house.

c. Cause: Joe did not behave well in class.

Effect: The teacher sent him to the principal's office.

d. Cause: Caspian was disrespectful to his supervisor.

Effect: His boss fired him.

e. Cause: Isla demonstrates good behaviour.

Effect: Her teacher gave her a gift.

f. Cause: Rumi hit a member of the group.

Effect: The leader expelled her.

Effect: The manager of the comedy club invited him

h. Cause: When water is heated.

Effect: It boils.

i. Cause: I forgot my lunch at home.

g. Cause: Finn is a funny performer.

Effect: I ate at the cafeteria

2. a. Red: Cara's dress is wrinkled.

Blue: Her Mother iron it.

b. Red: Sally wants to paint.

Blue: She took out her art box.

c. Red: There was a heavy snowfall.

Blue: There were no classes today.

d. Red: Soraya was exhausted.

Blue: She went to bed early.

e. Red: Xavier was very hungry.

Blue: He ate three hotdogs.

f. Red: Tatiana did not water her flowers.

Blue: They died.

g. Red: We ran out of milk.

Blue: We made hot chocolate with water.

h. Red: Whenever Atticus is around cats.

Blue: He sneezes.

i. Red: Zaylee could not see well.

Blue: She got glasses.

j. Red: The oven temperature was too high.

Blue: The cookies burned.

k. Red: Grandma is coming for dinner.

Blue: We cleaned the house.

l. Red: The popcorn bag ripped at the bottom.

Blue: The popcorn spilled all over.

m. Red:

m. Red: My cat is sick.

Blue: My mom took it to the vet.

n. Red: There is 30 cm of snow on the ground.

Blue: I made a snowman.

o. Red: Brody blew a giant bubble gum bubble.

Blue: It splattered on his face.

p. Red: Fletcher slipped on a banana peel.

B q. Red: My birthday.

Blue: My dad gave me a tablet.

r. Red: Eugene is sick.

Blue: He went to the doctor.

s. Red: To buy cheese.

Blue: Tabatha went to the grocery store.

t. Red: I poked a balloon with a needle.

Blue: It popped.

lue: He broke his leg.
u. Red: I pushed the power button of the remote control.

Blue: The T.V. turned on.

v. Red: I turned on the faucet.

Blue: Water came.

w. Red: Willow kecked her support worker at recess
Blue: She was not allowed in class.
3. Answers will vary.

a. He fell off the tree.

4. Answers will vary.

a. Because he wants to become an entrepreneur.

b. Because he does not want to borrow money to start his business.

c. Because he wants to advertise his business.

d. Because he posted the flyers in many places.

e. Because his business started to grow, and he needed support.

f. Because he knew how to treat animals.

g. Answers will vary.

5. Answers will vary.

a. Some bears retreat, others attack.

b. Some people want to touch it, others are afraid of it.

c. Some dogs growl at cats.

d. Cats hunt mice.

e. Mice eat cheese.

f. I would buy another one.

g. Answers will vary.

6. Answers will vary.

12. Elapsed Time – page 55

1.

1. 5 minutes.

2. 8:25

3. 10:30
4. 30 minutes.

5. 7:15

6. 30 minutes.

7. 35 minutes.

8. 1 and ½ hours.

9. 7:40.

10. 55 minutes.

11. 25 minutes.

12. 20 minutes.

13. 8:40.

15. 4 o'clock
16. 5:50.

17. 30 minutes.

18. 15 minutes.

19. 4:50.

20. 5:35.

21. 4:15.

22. 6 o'clock.

23. 30 minutes.

24. 1:20

25. 6:55

43. 1 hour and 40 minutes

2. 1. a. 1 hour and 30 minutes.

b. 1 hour and 40 minutes.

c. 1 hour and 50 minutes.

d. 1 hour and 30 minutes.

e. 1 hour and 15 minutes.

14. 8:55.

f. 1 hour and 15 minutes.
g. 1 hour and 45 minutes.

h. 1 hour and 10 minutes.

3. Answers will vary.
4. a. 15 minutes., 2 hours, 20 minutes. E.T. 2 hours and 35 minutes.

b. 12:35, 1:35, 2:10. E.T. 2 hours.

c. Answers will vary, but the elapsed time should be 2 hours and 35 minutes.
5. 1. 5:55.

2. a. 8:15.

b. 7:15.

c. 6:45.

3. a. 2:35.

b. 2:05.

c. 3:20.

d. 2:40.

4. a. 10:15.

b. 11:25

c. 10:25.

d. 11:10

13. Who Am I? – page 69

1. b. 2. a. 3. c. 4. b. 5. c.

6. a. 7. c. 8. b. 9. c. 10. a.
14. 5 Ws and H – page 70

1. a to h: Answers will vary.

2. a.

Who: Skyler.

Where: Whistler.

When: On the weekend.

What: Was afraid of crashing.

Why: Going down too fast.

How: He did a snowplow turn.

b. Who: Nia's dog

Where: Her home.

When: When she got home.

What: He wags his tail.

Why: He was happy to see her.

How: friendly.
c. Who: Juelz.

Where: Gym.

When: Yesterday.

What: He went to the gym.

Why: He wanted to be fit.

How: He paid with his credit card.

d. Who: I

Where: To the riding ring.

When: This morning.

What: To exercise my horse.

Why: He is overweight.

How: 1 hour every day

15. Unscramble – page 74

A. 1. Lucy Montgomery wrote Anne of Green Gables in 1905,

using some of her own life experiences in the story. Like Anne, s

he was born in eastern Canada and became an orphan when she was young.

Her father sent her to live with her grandparents in Cavendish, P.E.I.

2. They were both born in eastern Canada, they were orphans, and they lived in P.E.I.

3. Answers will vary.

B. 1. Theodore Seuss Geisel was born on March 2, 1904, in Springfield, Massachusetts.

His dream was to become a professor, but he decided to become a cartoonist after finishing

 university. After the Second World War, he started to write children's books.

However, his first book was rejected twenty-seven times before being accepted by a publisher.

 After that, he wrote more than sixty books. Dr. Seuss died on September 24, 1991.

2. A professor.

3. After finishing university.

4. 1945.

5. Twenty-seven times.

6. Answers may vary.

C. 1. I will never forget my first trip to Disneyland.

First, we went to see Mickey Mouse.

My sister and I took a picture with him.

Then we sat in front of the Magical Castle.

Finally, we had dinner together.

My family and I had a wonderful time.

2. In the morning, I go to the kitchen to have breakfast.

Firstly, I pour myself a bowl of cereal.

Second, I add milk to it.

Thirdly, I grab a spoon to eat the cereal.

Finally, I rinse the bowl and put it in the dishwasher.

16. Expository Writing – page 78

Answers will vary.

17. Planet Earth – page 81

1. Answers will vary.

E.g. It is a planet.

2. It is round.

3. c 4. d 5. b

6. The Arctic, Southern, Indian, Atlantic and Pacific.

7. c 8. c

9. Africa, Antarctica, Asia, Australia/Oceania, Europe, North America, and South America

10. d

11. b

12. Language

13. Country

14. a

15. Answer will vary.

16. Answer will vary.

17. Answer will vary.

18. Answer will vary.

19. Answer will vary.

20. Ottawa.

21. Answer will vary.

22. Answer will vary.

18. Characterization – page 86

1. Celest is a hardworking girl. She is dedicated

to playing the piano and to school.

She wants to be ready for the concert,

 so she will not make any mistakes.

2. Rodolph was disrespectful and obnoxious.

3. Giunia is kind, thankful, and generous.

4. Butch is loving and grateful.

5. Milena is shy and insecure.

6. Faye is caring and giving.

7. Brody is rude. And disrespectful.

8. Leia is bossy and demanding.

9. Sasha is caring and generous.

10. Agape is passionate and sensitive.

11. Rawan is respectful and loving.

12. Ramona is hardworking and patient.

13. Moriah is compassionate and unselfish.

14. Waiola is considerate and outgoing.

15. Tao is shy and reserved.

16. Cyprus is loving and caring.

17. Moraine is considerate and thoughtful.

18. 18. Atlas is rude and disrespectful.

19. Orion is timid and loving.

20. Raine is hardworking and skillful.

21. Ragnar is impolite and opinionated.

22. Ebony is proud and disrespectful.

23. Brodie is rude and thoughtless.

24. Morena is a conceit perfectionist.

25. Boyd is lazy and irresponsible.

26. Rhionna is helpful and considerate

19. Inferences – page 91

1. a. The window was broken with the baseball ball.

b. Mr. Earp found the baseball near the broken glass.

c. He was probably playing outside or hiding from his dad.

d. Mr. Earp called him, but there was no answer.

2. a. She lives on a ranch or a farm.

b. The text talks about a horse and a barn.

c. Because it is going to rain.

d. She noticed dark clouds and heard the thunder roll.

3. c   4. a 5. a 6. b 7. a

8. b   9. b   10. b   11. a   12. b

13. b   14. a   15. b   16. b

17. a   18. a   19. b

20. Drawing Conclusion – page 96

1. a. The Old girl's daughter.

b. morning

c. Breakfast

d. Catriona's mother

e. The mother.

f. It was her birthday.

g. Catriona's mom wanted to surprise

her with a nice breakfast for her birthday.

2. a. Faith

b. In the playground.

c. Calista

d. Calista already went home, and Faith will not be in

school the next day.

e. She is a caring and responsible friend.

3. a. Evening.

b. She lit the candle because it was dark.

c. Historical times.

d. the text mention candle, that she went outside to get

water from the well, and she took a sponge bath.

e. She probably lives alone, is hardworking and likes to read.

4. a. He will walk.

b. His wife or girlfried.

c. They kissed on the lips and he said, "I love you".

5. a. It is winter on a farm.

21. Conclusion from images – page 100

Answers will vary.

22. Predicting – page 102

1. a. The rain will get the foor wet.

b. His mom told him to close the window because it

could rain.

2. a. He will fall.

b. Because he lost his balance.

3. a. The cookies will burn.

b. She went to her bedroom and forgot about it.

4. a. He will pass the exam.

b. Because he spent time studying.

5. a. The puppy will jump in the pool.

b. The pappy ran towards the pool.

6. a. He will slipp and fall.

b. The floor was wet, and he was not careful because

he did not see the sign.

7. a. The vase will fall from the pedestal and brake on the floor.

b. Because she hit the pedestal with her feet.

8. a. Ruella will start eating the roasted meat.

b. Ruella jumped on the counter where Mrs. Burnaby left the roasted meat.

9. a. Pablo will buy a bicycle.

b. He took the money he received from his birthday and went

to the bike store.

10. a. Hallie will go to ballet class.

b. She placed her leotard and pointe shoe in the backpack.

23. Irony – page 106

A. 1. We would expect that a restaurant owner would know how to cook.

2. She cleans other people's houses but not her place.

3. We would expect that firefighters would keep their buildings safe.

4. The job of traffic officers is to issue parking tickets to other drivers.

If they get a ticket, it could mean that they don't take their job seriously

5. Pilots spend most of their work time up in the **air.**

6. We presume that the ice-cream was hard and

not soft as usual.

7. To wish someone to break a leg is like wishing good luck.

8. Jan meant that the river was filthy.

9. Mary is not a great singer.

10. When someone gives directions, we expect them to be

straightforward and easy to follow.

24. Sarcasm – page 108

A. 1. Nara's mother expected her to clean the house.

2. A person cannot have a wonderful day after crashing a car and losing a job.

3. Veronica did not enjoy the weekend because of the weather.

4. The lemonade was too sweet.

5. I wish Christmas break would be longer because I don't was to go back to school.

6. Roan was reprimanding himself for spilling the milk.

7. Lorna's brother was not happy that she dropped the laptop.

8. Conroy's girlfriend thinks that snakes are ugly.

B. a. 1. Millicent frowned

2. Millicent threw her arms up.

b. Answers may vary.

c. No. Millicent used words that express care and encouragement at

the same time that she was frowning, throwing her arms up and huffing.

d. 2.

e. "Opal, I am doing my best to help you, so can you please pay attention

to what I am saying?"

f. No.

25. Sentence Writing – page 111

1. Answers will vary – page 111

a. Ben does not like to drive to work; he prefers to take the C-train.

2. Answers will vary – page 112

258

a. Jill will be part of a fundraising event, so,

she decided to make candied apples to sell.

3. Answers will vary – page 115

a. Josh went to the mall to buy new sunglasses.

4. Answers will vary – page 117

5. Answers will vary – page 118

E.g. "I think Mr. Bruster is a nice man," said Jane.

6. Page 119

a. A five-star-hotel.

b. Part-time job.

c. Brand-new computer.

d. Worn-out shirt.

e. A good-looking girl.

f. A grayed-hair man.

g. A well-behaved kid.

h. A blue-eyed dog.

i. First-born child.

j. A long-legged player.

7. Answers will vary. – page 119

1. I bought a chocolate-covered caramel cake

for my birthday party.

8. Answers will vary – page 121

a. I sent him an email with the <u>homework</u>
assignment

attached to it. <u>It is due tomorrow.</u>

9. Answers will vary – page 123

a. The storm grew, gaining power with every
passing hour.

The farmer worried that it would damage his crops.

10. Answers will vary – page 125

a. When I looked up, my jaw dropped because up on
the tree

was the biggest cat I have ever seen.

11. Answers may vary – page 126

1. Marathon, pain, even though.

Kevin ran the marathon even though he had pain.

12. Answers will vary – page 127

1. <u>After</u> we heard the thunder, we decided to go
back to the hotel.

13. Answers will vary – page 128

14. Answers will vary – page 131

E.g. 1. Benji opened the door to greet the caller.

He invited the guest to come inside.

They chatted in the living room for a while.

2. But first, he went to the concession stand to buy
popcorn.

3. She started shivering.

4. He wiped it with a cloth.

5. She made her bed, went to the washroom and
changed. Etc

15. Answers may vary – page 137

1. Even though he is rich, he drives an old car.

16. Answers may vary – page 138

E.g. Draw a vehicle parked in front of a house.

Sentence: My dad parked his vehicle in front of our
house.

17. page 139

a. although

b. because

c. but.

d. However

e. despite.

f. So.

g. and

h. regardless

i. Although.

j. during.

k. regardless.

l. therefore.

m. because

n. and

o. so

p. During.

q. Despite.

r. However.

s. Regardless.

18. Answers will vary – page 140

a. This will cost me an arm and a leg, but I will buy
it anyway.

"An arm and a leg" is used to describe something
costly.

b. I am going to bed.

c. Holding a grudge and having an unpleasant
attitude .

d. Keep on trying, don't give up.

e. In extremily rare occasion.

f.Regret something that can't be changed.

g. Admiting defeat.

h.Call me any time.

i. It will happened very soon.

j. I don't know what is happening.

k. Heavy rain.

l. Easy.

m. Crocodile tears.

19. Answers will vary page 142

a.Books were piled on the coffee table, but Romy
had no desire to study.

b. While dad cooked <u>dinner,</u>

<u>Mom and I set the table.</u>

c. Gently, she <u>took his elbow</u>

<u>and led him to the house.</u>

d. Unfortunately, Mariela <u>failed the driving test.</u>

<u>She did not practice enough.</u>

e. An elegant dress <u>was hanging in the shop
window.</u>

<u>It was long, made of lavender brocade with a floral
design.</u>

f. The girl struggled <u>with math class.</u>

<u>Her mother thought it would be good to hire a tutor.</u>

g. It had been raining for two weeks straight.

The river began to rise.

h. I walked to the shed where I had left the pitchfork.

My dad still needed it to lift the rest of the hay.

i. Reading a book is like travelling in space and time.

There is no limitation to creativity.

j. The mist over the river was rising.

Soon, the fog was all around us.

20. Answers will vary – page 143

a. *Summer* is my favourite season of the year. The weather is warm,

I don't have to worry about homework, and there are endless outdoor's activities.

All the seasons are beautiful, but I am always looking forward to *summer*.

21. page 143

1. The sanke slithered on the grass this morning.

2. Animals are protected by law these days.

3. During the robbery at the store, Blimey sounded the alarm.

4. Beulah danced all night at the club.

5. Boris and his brother Bryan.

They love baseball.

They want to try out for the basketball team.

Every day.

They practice.

At the gym and in their driveway

22. A. 1. They walked the dog.

2. They finished their homework.

B. 1. They went to see the tigers.

2. They went to see the tigers.

c. 1. None.

26. Let's look at nature – page 146

1. Lighter.

2. It is short. It measures no more than 5 cm.

3. Only one, the hummingbird.

4. They drink the nectar of flowers and bird feeders.

5. Red.

6. Hummingbirds are attracted to this colour.

27. Fantasy or Fiction – page 148

A. 1. a   2. b.   3. b.

4. Answers will vary.

B. 1. b   2. a   3. a

4. Answers will vary.

28. Homographs – page 150

Clear:

1. The day is clear and frosty.

2. Do I make myself clear?

3. I need to clear my desk.

Bat:

1. My dad gave me a baseball bat.

2. There are many species of bats.

3. He didn't bat an eye when I called him out.

Fair:

1. You are not fair.

2. Michel has fair skin.

3. Mom went to the book fair last night.

Fine:

1. . Paul is a fine young man.

2. I paid a fine for a parking violation.

3. She has such fine hair!

29. Let's talk about things - 151

1. Soccer.

a. Answers will vary.

b. Answers will vary.

c. Soccer jersey, shorts, stockings, shin guards and shoes.

d. Answers will vary.

2. Cars

a to 6 Answers will vary.

3. Weather.

a to g Answers will vary.

4. Temperature.

1. By using a thermometer.

2. Celsius and Fahrenheit

3. Answers will vary.

4. 0C and 3F.

5. 100C and 212 F.

30. Wide Range – page 154

1. to 7. Answers will vary.

8. a They are professions

31. Compare and Contrast.

1. to 16. Answers will vary.

E.g. Bear and Moose:

Bear - Different: Bears are omnivores.

Moose – Different: Moose are Herbivores.

Alike: They are both wild animals.

32. What's next? – page 160

Answers will vary. E.g.

1. He fell to the ground.

2. He climbed the tree and placed the baby bird in the nest.

3. Melania began to play and sing.

4. He walked to school.

5. The door opened, and she climbed in.

33. Retelling a story page 161

1. a. to e. Answers will vary.

2. a. to d. Answers will vary.

3. 1. to 6. Answers will vary.

4. Answers will vary.

5. 1. Jim asked Martha if she was going to the playground.

2. Mother said that she is going to the mall to buy a new pair of shoes.

3. Owen asked Joel why he needed to go to his cousin's house.

4. I said to Stephen that I need t buy flowers for my mom.

5. Joel asked Laura if she could feed his horse over the weekend.

6. Rachel asked Ben if he wanted to go over for supper.

7. Julia said to Giovanna that she thinks that Hazel is an adorable child.

8. My teacher told me to let her know if I need more time to finish my homework.

9. Ruth said to Claudia that Mamma Mia is her favourite restaurant in town.

10. Dad told me to do my homework and clean my room when I get home.

11. My friend asked if we could order Chinese food for dinner.

12. Rupert said that he does not want to go skiing.

13. Leonel said that his favourite sport is soccer.

14. Marvin said that he was not sure if he wanted to buy that toy.

15. Lois said to Lorna that Hip-Hop is better than pop music.

16. Thomas yelled at his sister to not touch his video game.

17. Mirna asked Molly what time she is coming to play.

18. He said that she is beautiful.

19. Noemi said to Lena that he loved her but that she does not care.

20. Martin said that he is going to Jen's house tonight.

21. Joel thinks that it is a good idea to take Lucy with them.

22. Matt asked if Gina was ok.

23. Mira said to Moira that she could come to her house anytime she wanted.

24. Kaira asked the waitress for a piece of cake.

25. Dad said to Brian that he could go outside but only until supper time.

34. Reading Comprehension – page 170

A. Recall

1. a. Ottawa

b. Ottawa is the capital of Canada, located in the province of Ontario.

2. a. Canada's population.

b. Over 80% of the Canadian population lives near the United State border.

3. a. Canada's forested land.

b. It makes nearly 9% of the world's total area.

4. a. Canada's lakes.

b. Canada has more lakes than the rest of the world combined, and

that the largest lake in Canada is Lake Superior.

5. a. Indigenous people.

b. They have been in Canada for centuries.

6.a. Canada's national languages.

b. The national languages are English and French, but French

is the official language

only of Quebec and New Brunswick.

B. Sentence By Sentence – page 172

1. These sentences are about the origin and meaning of the name Canada.

2. These sentences are about the western provinces of Canada.

They are

Manitoba, Saskatchewan, Alberta, and British Columbia.

3. These sentences tell us that more than half of the Canadian

population live between

Ontario and Quebec.

4. These sentences inform us that the Canadian Atlantic provinces are

famous for fishing and

Mining.

C. Compare texts

A. Self-control 1.

1. b   2. a   3. a   4. b

5. a   6. b

B. Self-control 2.

1. a   2. b   3. a   4. b   5. c

D. What is the setting?

1. Morning dawn.

2. Winter in the country.

3. Ocean.

4. Night-time.

5. Afternoon.

E. The microwave.

1. The invention of the microwave.

2. He invented the microwave.

3. Engineer.

4. To feed it to squirrels during his lunch break.

5. The candy bar started to warm up and melt in his pocket.

F. Main Idea.

1.Margie enjoys reading.

2. Dorothy does not like dogs.

3.There was a snowstorm.

4. Crocodiles have a strong bite.

5. Dinosours were large animals.

6. c.   7. a.   8. b.   9. c.

35. Reading Comprehension – Moral stories – page 179

1. The Teddy bear.

a. He worked in the lobby of a hotel.

b. Because she had lost her teddy bear.

c. Yes, the manager and the chambermaid.

d. He went to the hotel's laundry room.

e. Between some bedsheets.

f. Hours.

g. She was tired of crying and waiting.

h. She was delighted and thankful.

i. She took a picture of the young man with his daughter and asked permission to use it.

j. Answer will vary.

k. Yes, she owned the chain of toy stores.

l. She made posters and placed them in all her stores.

m. Answer will vary.

n. Answer will vary. E.g. Probably not.

o. Answer will vary.

2. The neighbours.

a. Answer will vary. E.g. Lack of interest.

b. She thought that they had nothing in common.

c. She did not want him to bother her again.

d. They decided to buy another ball instead of arguing with the lady.

e. Her mother fell and needed help.

f. They went to Janette's house and decided to call an ambulance.

g. Their neighbour, with whom they never tried to have a relationship.

h. He was kind.

i. Embarrassed.

j. Answer will vary.

k. Answer will vary.

36. Find two things in the text – page 185

1. a. They are sisters.

b. To look at the grass covered with hail.

2. a. Two.

b. The text does not say.

37. Read and Draw – page 186

a. to l. Answers will vary.

38. Create an image – page 192

A. Answers will vary.

39. Skim and scan – page 193

1. to 5. Answers will vary.

40. Pronoun reverse – page 195

1. She.

2. she, They, our.

3. They, their.

4. He.

5. I, her, I.

6. She, her, They, her.

7. her, they, she.

8. It, their.

9. They, It.

10. He, They, his.

11. They, her. She, them.

12. us

13. We.

14. them.

15. it.

16. their.

17. he.

18. They.

19. They.

20. them.

21. He.

22. I.

23. Our.

24. them.

25. them.

26. I, me, it, my, hers (his).

27. We, our, we.

28. They.

29. we.

30. he, them.

41. Odd one out – page 197

1. c 2. b 3. c 4. b 5. c

6. b 7. a 8. d 9. c 10. c

11. b 12. a 13. d 14. b 15. a

16. d 17. c 18. d 19. a 20. d

21. d 22. a 23. b 24. b 25. c

26. d 27. c 28. b 29. b 30. b

42. What is that sound? – page 203

Answers will vary.

43. Put it in order – page 204

1. Answers will vary.

44. Fill in the blanks – page 205

A. 1. b 2. c 3. c 4. b 5. b

6. a 7. a 8. b 9. c 10. b

11. c 12. b 13. c 14. a 15. a

16. c 17. a 18. c 19. a

B. 1. If, she would

2. If.

3. If.

4. If, I would.

5. if

6. would have, if.

7. If, will

8. If, would not.

9. If, would not.

10. If, will not.

C. Answers will vary

45. Where Would You Go? – page 209

1. b. Nakiska

2. b. A hill at the park

3. a. The Atlantic Ocean

4. c. Lake Louise

5. b. Museum

6. c. Safari

7. c. NASA

8. a. New York City

46. Follow Directions – page 211

47. Creative writing – page 215

Answers will vary.

48. Creative thinking – page 220

Answers will vary.

49. Multipurpose – page 222

Answers will vary.

50. Skills – page 224

Answers will vary.

51. First Aid and emergencies – page 225

A. 1. To be safe means to be protected from harm and

To be prepared for emergencies.

2. An emergency is a serious situation that

happens when we do not expect, and requires

immediate attention.

3. Answers will vary.

4. First responders are professionals trained

to aid during an emergency. They are the police,

firefighters, and paramedics.

5. Call 911, and help with first aid skills.

B. 1. Answers will vary.

2. Answers will vary.

3.As little as two minutes from the time the smoke alarm sounds.

4. We may call 911 anytime but only when

people are injured, in danger,

due to sickness, accidents, or disasters.

C. First Aid Kit

D. 1. b

2. Clean the are with water or antiseptic spray, and

Cover it with an adhesive bandage.

3. a

4. a

5. to 10. Answers will vary

52. Sexual Harassmment – page 231

1. a   2. a   3. a   4. a

5. a   6. a   7. a

53. Good manners – page 233

1. a   2. b   3. a4. b   5. a

6. a   7. a

8. Answers will vary

9. c   10. a   11. a

54. Executive Functioning – page 235

1. Answers will vary

55. Types of decision – page 238

1. c   2. b   3. a   4. b   5. b

56. Would you rather – page 240

Fun:

1. to 10. Answers will vary.

(Serious, but fun)

57. Online research – page 243

A. 1. to 26. Answers available online.

1. to 9. Answers will vary

B. 1. to 8. Answers will vary

58. How many answers? – page247

a. to g. Answers will vary

59. Word play – page 249

1. Answers will vary.

60. Colour Play – page 255

Made in the USA
Middletown, DE
08 March 2021